Love Beckons

God's Gift of Prayer

Dr. Joyce Hajdukovic

outskirtspress
DENVER, COLORADO

Outskirts Press, Inc.
http://www.outskirtspress.com

ISBN: 978-1-4787-4997-4

Outskirts Press and the "OP" logo are trademarks belonging to Outskirts Press, Inc.

PRINTED IN THE UNITED STATES OF AMERICA

This book is lovingly dedicated to Teresa of Avila, a friend and guide. She has always been inspiring. May it be a fitting tribute on the occasion of her five hundredth birthday, March 28, 2015 and for as long as people benefit from these pages.

Contents

Acknowledgments

The great depth of the Christian life emerges with renewed vigor during these times of shifting cultural values. It is more than encouraging to see Christian leaders of differing traditions inviting all to the fullness of the Christian mystical life. Most noteworthy is the spiritual focus of Greek Orthodox theologian, John Zizioulas and Pope Benedict XVI. Their liturgical approach, fostering *communion* and *'sacramental mysticism' of the Eucharist* as the high point of union with God, will easily remind one of the well-known adage of Teilhard de Chardin, "All that rises must converge."

The average Christian, however, does not move in one straight line toward the permanent consciousness of *communion*. There are ups and downs, moments of light and darkness, all of which are considered in the simple developmental approach of Teresa of Avila. While it takes a trained eye to make the connections, once pointed out, people readily recognize their own experience in the pages of classical Christian literature and are more willing to persevere during the patches of dryness and darkness that all experience in prayer.

Those who benefit from these pages will offer thanks with me for the following contributions to this book, which was written over several years. First, we wish to thank the Rev. Dr. R. Gibbons of Oxford University in England for encouraging its publication in popular form.

Next, we are deeply grateful for the spiritual expertise and editorial advice of the Rev. Dr. M. Fuller of St. Mary of the Lake University in Mundelein, Illinois. This is very much our book and we are grateful for the many anonymous stories in it. Last but not least, we thank Evelyn Rachael Blacconeri for her complete financial funding of this project. Evelyn has also been more than generous in sharing her gifts with the Christian community in faith and service, especially as a helper catechist in Special Religious Education. As St. Paul remembered those closest to him, we can say regarding all of the above, "Our hearts give thanks with every thought of you."

Introduction

The mystical life is Christian life, which has, so to speak, become conscious of itself.

– Garrigou-Lagrange[1]

The Gospel of John promises the gift of *abiding union* for one who keeps the commandments. God's intimate presence is treated extensively in the epistles of John, especially in 1 John. The writings of Paul introduce us to the idea of the mystical body of Christ. We *are* that body. The personal experience of these biblical writers enables them to be open to the inspiration of the Word, which calls all of us to union with God. In view of the Incarnation, the invitation to *conscious union with God* appears to be a clearly Christian call. This book is an attempt to get beyond the prejudice concerning the mystical life which has grown up in past centuries through lack of a spiritual understanding of Scripture. Some have arrived at a moral understanding and many more at a literal understanding of Scripture. Slowly, there is a spiritual or mystical understanding evolving as Christianity becomes conscious of itself.

---

1   Garrigou-Lagrange, Reginald, O.P., *Christian Perfection and Contemplation,* (Rockford, Illinois: Tan Books, 2003) 128.

Human longing is gradually and ultimately fulfilled as a person becomes ready to receive God's gift of unconditional, transforming love. This gift is concretely presented to Christians in the person of Jesus, who is our very life. We become conscious of his transforming love in the developmental stages of our spiritual life. Following this inner journey in the lives of people, this presentation will remain true to both these real life stories as well as to the solid foundation provided in the classical writings of Teresa of Avila and John of the Cross.

Everyone is longing for love. Many of us look in the wrong places. Young people today are looking for an inner participation or connectedness in something, *they know not what.* Their search sounds very similar to that implied by these words found in our Christian mystics. The desire to live a spiritual life from within and not from something *imposed* from the outside is a valid position teaming with potential. The Christian mystics, Teresa of Avila and John of the Cross, have integrated a life motivated from within with rich exterior practice. Their teaching inspires people of all ages to seek *consciousness* of the profound inner life we have all been gifted with. The end result of a conscious union with God in the Christian tradition is necessarily *connectedness* with each other as well. Our God is one in community.

This author began her journey in faith as a high school student, simply because an insightful teacher left about writings from the Christian mystics. It is our hope that these pages will provide an inspiring example of the Christian mystical life as it is lived by ordinary people today. There has been a false notion that the Christian mystical life is all about phenomenal experience. That is far from the truth. The Christian mystical life is, in fact, about our intimate life with Christ, who brings us into the love of God the Father through the outpouring of their Holy Spirit. It is all about the experience of this unconditional love and our response. When we experience God's love as persons, we want to return it and to share it with others.

Often we are *not conscious* of love as the focal point of the Christian life. Still, it is an experience for which we long. When God is not the source, many false attempts are made in its pursuit. We become broken, psychologically wounded. Experts in the field of psychology help pick up the pieces, but then another set of false attempts follow. We begin here from a different place, from the presupposition that *God is Love* (Jn 14:20). The not so obvious consequence is that Jesus wished us to be one, *as* He and the Father are one (Jn 17:21). This is a call for each of us to an *intimately spiritual union* with God and others. A confirmation student once wanted to be sure that this approach would not leave her *missing out* on the good things of this world. By the end of class she was convinced that starting with a superficial focus was what *would indeed* be her demise.

If young people reject the Scripture today, could it be that the presentation of it has not been on the spiritual or mystical level? One gets the impression that they are tired of a "moral pounding" on their person, which does not allow them to be virtuous from a deeply personal experience of union with God. They tend to *know* if one is speaking from experience. We do much good for those around us by giving ourselves time to *experience* union with God. The Holy Spirit desires it even more than we do.

This union of the created spirit with uncreated Spirit, is the essence of the Christian mystical life. It is Christianity becoming conscious of its *true self.* It is not, as some would have us believe, the gift that God gives only to a few rare saints. This opinion, as it had been taught in the past, waters down our Christian faith and makes it impossible for us as humans to think we can actually attain to an experience of intimate love *in God* without being extraordinary. Returning to the basic Christian teaching regarding baptism, we see that the Father, Son and Holy Spirit *live in* each of us. It is a *mutual treasure.* What an experience it is when Christians meet on this level of appreciation.

A consciousness of the pure love in which we long to participate comes only when much of the self-fulfilling ego has been stripped from the surface of our awareness. Once beyond the self we can grow from glory to glory into that love in which and for which we were created. It is this happiness which we as human beings desire, not knowing sometimes why we are continually dissatisfied. Deep interiority beckons, *like a wind tunnel,* drawing us into the original innocence and core consciousness by which we intuitively know *the face of God* as the place to which we can return for happiness.

Teresa of Avila at first envisioned the soul as a beautiful crystal castle with her focus on the Lord at its center. However, when she began to write she was reminded of the famous Alcazar found in Segovia. There is only one castle in the world like it. Teresa and John of the Cross traveled through Segovia making foundations. John worked on buildings for his discalced friars with his brother, Francisco. He was once known to say that they would build *another alcazar.* Knowing his penchant for simplicity and poverty, it is easy to see it was only in jest. He did most likely mean that they would build a place where the fullness of the interior journey could be arrived at simply and completely.

Bringing the desire for an interior life closer to our time, Evelyn Underhill explains how in our current evolution of the person, one is more inclined to be open to a theology of immanence or *indwelling presence* rather than one emphasizing sin. She explains the importance of dogma along with personal experience so that one does not fall into pantheism. In the story of Clare, in chapter five, there will be an example of personal experience and dogma, showing how these easily fit together. Starting from experience, Underhill holds out this unforgettable reality: "The Absolute Whom all seek... stands as it were at the very threshold of consciousness and knocks, awaiting the soul's slow discovery of her treasures."[2] Teresa's presentation in *The Interior Castle* is simple because the focus is on *the treasure within.* Everyone has this treasure. Focusing on it is what makes the mystic.

Beginning with creation, as seen in *Genesis,* the Christian tradition holds that all persons are created for an intimate relationship with God and each other. The path back to original innocence can be found on our journey, using opportunities for Christian contemplative prayer. In this original state, all of creation worked together in the unity of love. From the time of Moses, who talked with God regularly, until the

---

2   Evelyn Underhill, *Mysticism: A Study in the Nature and Development of Man's Spiritual Consciousness* (New York: E.P. Dutton, 1930),99.

present day, we have a clear record of how personal union with God was sought and achieved. The presence of God is operative in a significant way in human beings, especially as they become conscious of their longing for a union in love. Since there is no time in God even Old Testament mystics received the grace of union with God through the Word, who had not as yet become man. Thomas Merton taught that the desire is given before the gift itself. God never gives a desire without purifying us and preparing us to receive it. The gift of union with God is truly a worthy object of our longing.

In his *Toward a Psychology of Being* Abraham Maslow holds that transcendence is needed for a person to become a mature adult. Yet, the psychology of personality is not able to help us achieve what is needed *for permanent transcendence.* Even when we are not paying attention, we may experience the *awakenings* which Maslow speaks of. But what do we do with them? How do we dispose ourselves for where they are meant to lead? And how do we allow them to become a permanent part of our consciousness? We will find these answers in the developmental process of Teresa's *Interior Castle.* In this classic work she outlines a developmental process in which the *awakenings of God's love,* from the core of our being, transform all the aspects of life from the inside out.

A taste of transcendence can be easily dissipated and forgotten. However, a complete and lasting transformation of our consciousness is the gift of God given in prayer. This begins with an awareness of the divine indwelling and a spirit of recollection. Teresa tells us that in recollection we draw our faculties inward to focus on the Object of our desire. Our longing for *genuine love* in relationship cannot be fully achieved by psychology or philosophy alone. Arriving at it requires that the selfish element of the personality be cleared away by a means not entirely at our disposal. As wounded human beings, transformation is a gift that God gives, often along with or soon after the desire for it. This desire must be real. One must be willing to let go of things such as the *masked* existence of our persona. This as well as what the culture around us deems as important becomes an obstacle to the union we seek. Often people go from project to project or from relationship to relationship without realizing why they are not happy. In Teresa of Avila and other Christian mystics the starting place for human dignity is in the *divine indwelling*, a resource beyond the scope of psychology and philosophy.

Before the science of psychology and its obsession with human relationship evolved to its present pitch, there lived this sixteenth century nun, Teresa of Avila, who became known as an expert in the psychology of relationship. The method of Teresa of Avila is simple. She gets straight to the point of human dignity. It is the gift of God within, beckoning at the very depths of each human being. In response to this call Teresa's *Interior Castle* presses on toward the center of human consciousness with single minded focus.

When Teresa was given the task to write about prayer she prayed fervently to be able to explain what she knew about it from her own experience. She believed that to experience contemplation and to be able to say anything about it are two separate gifts. Each is valuable. As these stories will show, Teresa's insights speak to the religious experience of many today. They enable us to appreciate the gift of prayer that God has blessed us with. In our busy lives, if this is not clearly pointed out, God's invitation will be lost. Teresa was called upon both to be a contemplative and to teach us about it even now, five hundred years later.

As has been said, Teresa used a castle she had seen, the Alcazar of Segovia, as the model for her writing. Around this castle her words drew a picture for us of a slimy mote with many evil creatures in it. These dark influences would attempt to keep us in their murky environment and out of the castle. The security of the castle would provide us with interiority as a path leading to personal, conscious union with God. She saw prayer as the door to the castle, leading to deepening interiority. The mercy of God allowed one to overcome the evils on the outside and to enter the castle of the soul by means of prayer. Reflecting on one's personal dignity as the dwelling place of God would be the means of recollection by which one could make most progress through its "many dwelling places: some up above, others below, others to the sides; and in the center and middle is the main dwelling place, where the very secret exchanges between God and the soul take place."[3]

The charm of Teresa's writing is that her focus is clear. It is on the Lord at the center of the castle. He is more available than we think. God abides at the very center of our being and is closer to us than we are to ourselves. Teresa keeps reminding us not to look for love in other places. She is fond of speaking of the search of St. Augustine who looked everyplace and finally found God within. So Teresa takes us on a journey, a spiritual pilgrimage as it were, patiently showing us by a slow developmental process how to allow the layers of our resistance to be melted away by God's love. The dust we collect which mars the beauty of our diamond, the human soul, must be removed to allow the bright light of love within to shine forth.

Teresa starts by speaking of the outside of the castle, which is the human soul and God's temple. She encourages us to focus, not on the outer setting of the diamond, but on its inner beauty. She maintains that *everyone* is as capable of enjoying God's presence within as a crystal is naturally capable of reflecting the rays of the sun. Yet, those who do not believe in this favor God is most willing to give, will have no experience of it. "For God does not like us to put a limit on His works."[4]

When our concerns become self-centered even the pious thoughts we had of God or of serving others run out of fuel. How God's gift of love, known by Christians as the Holy Spirit, beckons us to perfect our human love is the story of Teresa of Avila's *Interior Castle*. Each one of us is that beautiful, many faceted castle, which houses the God of heaven and earth at our center. However, few of us are consciously present at the center of things with God, in the love which has the power to mutually delight us.

The purpose of this book is to show through the lives of ordinary Christians living today how God's action within enables them to relate in ways that satisfy their deepest longing for the receiving and giving of

---

3   Teresa of Avila, *The Interior Castle in the Classics of Western Spirituality*, trans. Kieran Kavanaugh and
     Otilio Rodruquez (New Jersey: Paulist Press, 1979),36.
4   Ibid., 37.

love. It is no secret that the more our love is perfected the better we humans are at more stable relationships. Yet, we cannot perfect ourselves by ourselves. We get so far and that is it. We allow the divine action to take over, or we tend to go backwards.

The true stories told here reflect the magnificent rays of love transforming each of the persons who were open to love's call. These stories depict the action of God as well as a personal response to God's invitation to grow deeper in love. While protecting the identity of the individuals involved in all of these stories, the spiritual events are true and most of the people involved in them are still among us. May these events be a concrete depiction for our readers of the *living water* as it becomes effective as the source of good works, the transition to contemplation, the union of our entire being in God, the purification of our faculties and ultimately, our ascent into the mystery of God.

1

Leaving the Mote

There will be no full interior life of love with God or anyone else until a person gets out of the mote. Our first story therefore, begins in the mote. It is the story of a brave Christian woman who wished her story to be told so that others might have hope. For this reason we agreed that we would call her Espiranza, which means hope. Espiranza's story is about leaving the mote, a place of evil she found herself in and from which she had a hard time leaving. Her human longing for pure love was very great. Even greater than the evil she found herself drowning in. Eventually, Espiranza found the door to the castle, which was prayer. It became her greatest asset in entering the first dwelling places described by Teresa of Avila. Espiranza also took every human means to overcome her difficulty. Hers is a story that proves that contemplatives are not people removed from the problems of the world. Sometimes the answers are to be found when people are guided to ask the right questions.

More and more the science of philosophy and psychology lead us to ask the right questions. However, as we have noted in the introduction, these fields do have boundaries which prevent one from arriving at the consciousness of the stable solutions we seek. It is the love of original innocence in which we each looked at the face of God before we were born. This face of pure love is the object of our longing. Throughout

Scripture one runs across the theme "We long to see your face." Yet, we are told that it is impossible to see the face of God and live. Teresa solves the paradox. Patiently, we must work our way through *The Interior Castle* where *seeing* is not a matter of the senses, but is a matter of *knowing* with purified faculties. We can observe the story of our own soul, the Christian soul, gradually becoming conscious of itself in its transformed state as a dwelling where the movement of God's love takes place. Christ's love is constantly received and is simultaneously poured out in works that are not one's own. When thinking of good works Teresa clearly knew that none of them have their principle in ourselves. Rather, the source of our good deeds are in *the fount* in which we are planted, receiving warmth and light from the inner dynamism of God's love.[5] This is the first time we encounter God's love *as living water in the Interior Castle.* It is described as the source of good works in the first dwelling places.

Espiranza's Story

Moving from the mote to the first dwelling places of *The Interior Castle* was a very difficult process for Espiranza. You see, Espiranza was sexually abused as a child by a distant family member. She did not speak of it, but wondered if her siblings experienced the same treatment. Later she found out they had. The effects of this molestation had serious consequences for Espiranza. She became extremely promiscuous. At the same time she was very spiritual. She brought this condition to a spiritual director, who walked with her in spite of the fact that some would think it best to pursue therapy alone. The director saw the deepest part of Espiranza struggling to get free. There was an element in her that was not only spiritual, but bordered on the contemplative. The director cringed inside when Espiranza told how she would put a condom on the bible beside the bed of the married man she sought out for sex when she felt really down. Espiranza was not initially ready to receive God's gift of unconditional, transforming love. It would take some active work on her part as God gave her courage to

---

5   Ibid., 41.

follow through, seeking humble guidance from her doctors, therapists and a spiritual director.

After getting to know her spiritual director, it was decided between the two of them that Espiranza would seek therapy, but remain in close connection with the director as well. Several therapists were tried. It was not a smooth path. It seems the abused wear a sign on their foreheads saying 'available' and those who seek them out because of their vulnerability are the only ones who can read it. Many tear-filled nights were spent praying on the phone with her spiritual director.

Eventually, Espiranza adjusted very well to an expensive, but excellent woman therapist and received hormonal medication in addition to therapy. She was out of the mote in a relatively short time. Espiranza truly believes that her daily prayer was the real thing that cured her. Many of the themes in Teresa of Avila's first dwelling places come to fore in the story of Espiranza. Hers is a story of prayer, self-knowledge and dependence on the mercy of God.

The Door to the Castle Is Prayer [6]

Espiranza prayed often and intensely, alone and with her director, to be lifted out of the mote. When she finally knew her cure was permanent, Espiranza continued the spiritual practices she had never really given up. Being Catholic, she attended Mass frequently and had an exceptional love for Eucharistic Adoration. She found peace in centering prayer. She joined others her age in spiritual practices, and was often chosen as a leader.

Today Espiranza is married with children of her own. She protects them with a passion from any form of abuse, and with her husband, leads programs for married couples. None would guess what her journey entailed. Espiranza is open to ministering to the sexually abused, if God should open up this possibility. Meantime, she encourages everyone to enter the door of the castle, intense prayer.

---

6   Ibid., 38.

Self - Knowledge

It is easy to see how self-knowledge played a role in the story of Espiranza. Without constant open dialogue with her spiritual director and legitimate counselors, the miracle of grace in this story may not have happened. Without careful reflection on what triggered her episodes of promiscuity, doctors would not have prescribed the medication most needed.

Teresa of Avila holds self-knowledge as a very important aspect throughout her spiritual masterpiece, *The Interior Castle*. As it deals farther on with some very advanced stages of prayer Teresa says, *Self-knowledge is the bread that must be eaten with every food, however dainty.*[7] From the beginning prayer of meditation, through the many stages of contemplation and to the transforming union with God that integrates it all, self-knowledge is recommended as 'the bread' that must be eaten. Self-knowledge for Teresa is not rooted in self, but in the awesome mystery of God's indwelling Spirit of love, giving humans a dignity beyond comprehension.

God's Mercy

Teresa probably did not know an *Espiranza*, but she did have experience of *back-sliding* in her own prayer life. For this reason she makes the whole developmental process of deep prayer a work of God's mercy. To the casual reader it would seem that Teresa humbled herself to quite an extent. There are a few reasons for this self-portrait. First, the Spanish Inquisition at the time not only rooted out heresies, but greatly scrutinized religious founders. Teresa's writings were questioned. *The Interior Castle* was hidden in an oven by her novices for fear it would be destroyed. Teresa thought that if she humbled herself first, she would not give her inquisitors a reason to do so. Second, it is a fact that when one moves on in the developmental stages of spiritual maturity Teresa outlines here, one really becomes humble to the degree that one advances.

Our Lord himself thought Teresa over did it with this false humility.

---

7   Teresa of Avila, *The Book of Her Life in The Collected Works of Teresa of Avila,*vol.1, trans. Kieran Kavanaugh and Otilio Rodriquez (Washington D. C.: ICS, 1987), 129-130.

Before she wrote *The Interior Castle* He inspired her not to focus so much on her unworthiness. Rather, to remember that she was *made in God's image*. Thus, seeing the human soul as a radiant castle reflecting God's light from its very center, Teresa taught a most positive spiritual theology - often overlooked in our busy culture.

The closer one gets to the center, the greater the light one sees reflected through the many facets of the soul. All the faculties and ministries of a person eventually become gloriously radiant with God's own light. God is known by Teresa as *His Majesty*, the King of the castle. When she speaks of the seventh dwelling places at the center of the castle, which is the human soul, she calls God, the *Lord of Glory*. It is here that a person participates most fully in the inner life of God and thereby is capable of the most intimate human relationships as well. The fulfilment of human longing for relationship, a connectedness with others that is permanent, requires a spotless diamond, which reflects the unconditional love of the Lord of Glory.

All of this is obviously God's work in us and not our own. Yet, Teresa is surprised here in the first dwelling places that we are taught only *about what we do* in prayer and not about *what the Lord does* in a soul. She asks us to be conscious *of Him at the center*. To turn our eyes there, rather than thinking of the dwelling places as being in a straight line each following in file after the other.[8] Thus our focus is immediately centered.

Rather than staying a long time in any one room of the castle, Teresa would have us moving around. The exception would be to remain in those dwelling places where self-knowledge is deepening.

> *For never, however exalted the soul may be, is anything else more fitting than self-knowledge...For humility, like the bee making honey in the beehive is always at work...Let the soul sometimes ponder the grandeur and majesty of its God. Here it will discover its lowliness better than by thinking of itself.[9]*

8   Kavanaugh, *Castle*, 42.
9   Ibid., 42-43.

Each year our adult bible class did something special for Pentecost. One particular year we discussed an article on the indwelling of the Holy Spirit. There was a relatively new member, quite devoted to her faith, who attended this faith sharing. Upon hearing that the God of heaven and earth, Father, Son and Holy Spirit lives in our hearts, in the depths of our souls, her eyes opened wide and the class fell silent. She admitted that in all her years practicing the faith she had never heard this before.

That the God of heaven and earth desires union with each of us and wishes to take delight in us in intimate mutual union while we are still alive on this earth is something unknown to most people. Yet, it is a main theme in the many 'abiding love' passages in John, especially in the epistle, First John. It is also found in the Spirit to spirit passages of St. Paul, quoted extensively by mystics. Because of our fascination with these topics, our Scripture class had often chosen to once again study the writings of John and Paul from different perspectives. These New Testament books are known as *high Christology*. They take us to that depth of spirit where capacity for the relationship every human longs for can take place.

Core relationship of a spiritual nature is the only kind that is permanent. When people relate from this depth of spirit they can truly say "Love is stronger than death." God, who is closer to us than we are to ourselves, can make this kind of connectedness happen as it involves Spirit to spirit relating. In this kind of union of uncreated Spirit to human spirit the Christian life becomes conscious of itself. It becomes the 'mystical life' Christians are called to in Baptism.

The study of *The Interior Castle* teaches us simplicity. Many times during our lifetime we are asked to let go of things or relationships, even religious experiences, that weigh us down, distracting us from God. This can happen when a person gets so tied up in their own experience of God and they forget or never have been told that *God is not our experience*. We may become attached to it as well as to other things. We are asked to desire union with God alone and to become ready for the action of the Holy Spirit within beyond our own expectations. In letting go and surrendering we receive much more and on a deeper level. This reminds one of the well-known passage, *Eye has not seen and ear has not heard what God has prepared for those who love him.* However, here in the first dwelling places of *The Interior Castle* the operation of God is still indirect. The Holy Spirit beckons through people, books, sermons and various external means such as the beauty in creation.

Indirect Operation of God - First Dwelling Places

In the first dwelling places the person has not as yet exhausted their human resources for psychological growth. The Holy Spirit assists the individual in self-help projects. Spiritual practices are of an active nature. In an unthreatening environment the beginner can reflect on the disparity between their ideals and lived experience. The person is doing their work with God's help. This is the way of beginners. It will progress until the end of the third dwelling places when, in transition, one will experience the first moments of God's direct action within.

All through the active stages of the spiritual pilgrimage, Teresa asks us to keep our eyes fixed toward the center where God dwells as in a paradise. It is a place we are called to reach in this life. It is a consciousness that transforms us and our human longings so that as God reaches out to us in beckoning love, we are able to reach back, in order to experience the stable connectedness for which we long.

Teresa's understanding of self-knowledge is very different from that of our secular world. It is not a self-grounded, but a God-grounded knowledge. Thus it has transformative power, which alone can enable us to reach what we most long for: connectedness and mutuality in love. Espiranza longed for a healthy connectedness, a true communication with others on every level. Eventually she found that a true stable relationship is rooted in God and sought her healing in prayer, humbly seeking assistance from others, whom she was willing to follow to her desired outcome.

Signposts - First Dwelling Places

In the first dwelling places one is newly converted to the interior life. There is the danger of falling back into the 'mote' or evil ways.

Prayer is infrequent and rote with many distractions. Spiritual guidance may be informal through moral friendships. Serious backsliding into the mote may be avoided with the help of clinical or pastoral guidance. Intense and regular prayer along with humbly facing the need for change are indispensable.

Spiritual Practices - First Dwelling Places

In the first dwelling places the focus is on the virtues, developing a regular prayer practice and remembering God's mercy during falls from grace. One will learn the prayer of active recollection during vocal prayer, paying attention to the One with whom we are speaking. Depending on one's denomination, the Sacrament of Reconciliation may be a powerful source of healing which enables one to refocus on original ideals and values.

Many self-help strategies may be used along with pastoral or psychological counseling as they are needed. It is a great advantage to become aware of God's growing role in prayer. If a person is to enter the second dwelling places, it is basic to become aware of unnecessary distractions as well as superficial attachments. Teresa teaches that this discernment of what is necessary for one's state in life is important to establish here in the very beginning, or else one may never reach the final dwelling places.

Conclusion

Entering the castle from a place of evil may be more dramatic than entering it from a more secure life. However, interiority must be learned in either case and so there is always a transition to a recollected or 'conscious' spiritual life. Many times, even the Christian life is not a conscious one. Baptism is hardly ever taught as a door to consciousness of God's indwelling presence. When approached in all honesty, this presencis presence holds the answer to all of our needs. God desires more than we know to become active in our lives. Sacraments as well as prayers often become things we do, not an awareness of the Other with whom we share a love relationship.

2

Spiritual Conversation

Conversation with self, others and God is a normal part of every Christian life. Our experience was in a Scripture study group which lasted over a period of twelve years. The group had a variety of people. Some were intent on learning all they could about the facts contained in Scripture. Most were open not only to the literal meaning of the text, but also to the moral and spiritual senses of God's Word. Members edified each other with the witness they gave in setting a good example for their families and in accepting the cross in their daily lives, especially that of problems with their children and illnesses.

After about two years or so, a small group within the class showed an attraction for *resting* in God's Word. This group simultaneously began meeting for contemplative prayer, first at a home of one of the members and then in the church. We will meet up with this group again in chapter four. For now we will continue with the topic of 'conversation' as it occurs most frequently in beginners on the way to union with God. It is normal for people to talk to themselves about themselves all day long. It is part of the ego *crud* that is gradually removed in a healthy spiritual life.

Hyacinth's Story

In the Scripture class after the exegesis of the text was presented, ideas were shared on how to begin conversing with others and God about matters of faith. The members were increasingly ready to receive the Word of God and to make it part of their lives on a variety of levels. Speakers were chosen who attended both the contemplative prayer group and the Scripture classes. The quality of their presentations depended largely on their own interior life as well as the desire and ability to put together a meaningful talk. One such speaker was Hyacinth. Hyacinth recognized *spiritual nakedness* as important for union with God. She was given the *Psalms of Lamentation* on which to speak. Now and then Hyacinth was called upon to present a topic that nobody else in the class could have given. This was such a time.

Hyacinth studied a paper on *The Dark Night* of John of the Cross and related it to the passages of the Old Testament Psalms which expressed devastation and even a feeling of abandonment. In some cases these reflected her own interior struggle, known only to her spiritual director. It felt to her like being suspended above a chasm without support and no idea of an outcome.

Hyacinth went on to explain that in the Old Testament times the prevailing idea was that the earth was flat with a watery chasm below it. Leviathan, a sea monster, was thought to prowl these treacherous waters known as *Sheol,* sometimes seen as an equivalent for our word *hell.* In the dark night, when the Holy Spirit knows one is ready, perceptions from the unconscious may emerge unannounced as did Leviathan from the watery depths of *Sheol.* John of the Cross explains this experience as a kind of *hell.* Hyacinth herself experienced the lines she quoted. She surrendered herself to God, even though this condition should last forever. And so the class went on. Hyacinth quoted Psalm 69: 2-3: "I am sinking in the deepest swamp, there is no foothold; I have stepped into deep water and the waves are washing over me. Worn out with calling, my throat is hoarse, my eyes are strained, looking for my God."

There is always a tendency to Christianize the psalms once their original meaning has been learned. Here we recall the words of Christ on the cross: "Father, into your hands I commend my spirit." This is a perfect lament, a line of courage and even comfort for anyone suffering interior trials. This part of Hyacinth's story is an example of how we look to those beyond us on the spiritual journey to find understanding of a deeper consciousness. Would that all Scripture teachers and scholars had a spiritual or mystical sense of Scripture. How rich the presentation of the Word would become if the application to daily life included our deepest consciousness as Christians.

Often we do not know with whom we may rub shoulders. We are not ourselves deep enough to listen intently or desire to know the full effect of the gifts of God which surround us in the consciousness of others. So it is very likely that some of what Hyacinth taught that day went over the heads of her hearers. Similarly, people don't mind studying *The Interior Castle* more than once. They feel they never really understood it all the first time. The classics are ageless and are around to be studied again and again.

Conversation with Self

Indicative of the beginner's interior spiritual climate is the constant dialogue with self. At the center of the beginner's world is the self, not the self which was created in God's image, but the self who is created in his own imagined importance. Flights of fancy which make up one's ordinary waking hours may extend even to the doing of good in which one's program, or ideas must encompass all. Since one is not in touch with this highest giftedness in God's grace, mere human intelligence, cleverness and cunning can become destructive. Everyone, but the person himself may realize that something is very wrong here. As one's sense of ministry evolves, one's best gift feeds the needs of the group one serves. The conversation with self is replaced with a dialogue that benefits the community.

The active prayer of recollection recommended by Teresa of Avila in the second dwelling places often corrects ego motivation before it has a chance to do harm to self or the ministry of others. Teresa's solution to the ego problem is simple, but powerful. Her directive is that as soon as one finds the mind unoccupied by anything important for one's state in life, one returns to the presence of God in whatever form seems best. This may be a word, phrase or image that makes one more conscious of God's presence than of oneself and personal imagined importance. "For His Majesty brings us to another stage ...and we shall enjoy many more blessings than we could have imagined...blessings experienced even in this lifetime."[10]

The Jesus Prayer, with its many forms, is an example of such a prayer of recollection. By constant repetition it trains the mind to refocus. The active prayer sentence of Father Thomas Keating, O.C.S.O. would be another example. In this form of *active recollection* one takes an inspiring phrase or sentence to return to throughout the day. Teresa recommends that the method one chooses be as short as possible, but she is not at all rigid about what it is to be. The simple word 'Jesus' suffices for the traditional Jesus Prayer, which originally is quite long.

The human soul is itself a place of solitude. Entering there, we can become as calm as a lighted candle, going out into our daily activities drawing from that inner source of life within, just as the candle draws from the wax that nourishes it. However, a person does not arrive at this kind of recollection instantly. It takes time and patience. Ordinarily persons learn to communicate with others about God before communicating with God throughout the entire day. Ministry flows powerfully from this consciousness of the presence of God. .

Conversation with Others

Consistent with her focus on relationship, Teresa puts a great emphasis on spiritual friendship and conversation. The emphasis for beginners is on friendship with the Lord and all other friendships which foster it. Her feeling that it is hard for one beset by so many dangers to be alone would be true even more so today. She suggests we surround ourselves, as much as possible, with persons of experience as only they can lead us to where they are. This is the entire thrust of our church today in its focus on *Evangelization,* a topic widely studied and discussed on the local level. False humility, which once was considered

---

10   *The Way of Perfection in the Collected Works of Teresa of Avila,* vol.2, Chapters 28-29, trans. Kieran Kavanaugh (Washington D.C.: ICS, 1980), 140-149.

virtue, calling us to bear silent witness to God, no longer works in a society where everyone speaks their mind. How to tactfully and boldly proclaim God's word was never a problem for the saints and now we all must consider becoming one of them. We are encouraged to share our faith not only in our small study groups, but with everyone. This may be a new approach, especially for those who would have previously considered evangelization the role of the clergy.

Spiritual Direction

Spiritual direction is a special kind of spiritual conversation where one person definitely has more experience and knowledge than the other. Those in the second dwelling places rarely recognize the person of a spiritual director, nor the need for one. The humility and wisdom to recognize this charism as important for oneself may come later, but Teresa's suggestion that we seek one with experience here in the second dwelling places leaves one open to think that even here spiritual direction may be sought. The experienced director may see in an individual case that the freedom to let go of disordered attachments will not be possible without the direct action of God. We cannot perfect ourselves by ourselves. Some deep seated habits require the direct action of God and the willingness of a person to allow it. When a person has done about all they can on their own, it is time for them to do more listening than talking in prayer.

On the other hand, a *person of experience* to the beginner may not be a spiritual director at all, but a companion who prays and attends liturgies regularly. It may be one who receives the sacraments regularly or understands the basic doctrines of the faith and practices them. It may be a pastor or pastoral counselor. Such are the friends Teresa encourages us to have at the beginning, in the first and second dwelling places.

Kevin Culligan, in his dissertation on Spiritual Direction, states the common problem of resistance that directors often face. "The major impediment to progress toward divine union is the failure of persons to abandon themselves to the guidance God gives them."[11] The reasons may be many. Let us not assume that it is always a lack of will. There may be no suitable directors available. Or one, not knowing its role, may fear the dark night. "Thus spiritual direction emerges…by which beginners and proficients in the spiritual life are assisted to overcome their resistance to God and to abandon themselves to His help."[12]

Conversation with God

Although Teresa consulted many theologians, she herself, had a hard time finding the method of recollection that would work for her until she discovered Francis Osuna's *Third Spiritual Alphabet.* We are told she practiced this method of active recollection for the rest of her life. With great flexibility, she would be a great model of the forms of 'centering prayer' practiced today. While Teresa did not have access to the entire bible as we do today, she carried sections of it in a pocket close to her heart. This way she felt she allowed the Word of God to penetrate her heart by a kind of osmosis.

Today there are many bibles, many translations available with study guides for a myriad of uses. Do these enable one to penetrate the Word and have the Word penetrate us with any greater advantage? Ultimately, it will take a *resting* in the Word, which some of the people in our Scripture class discovered. Meantime, Teresa advises that we simplify our prayer, using the Word of God in whatever form seems helpful. She herself always kept a spiritual book beside her as she knew that the heights of contemplation are not always possible and are beyond us to achieve for ourselves. She valued, above all, the prayer of recollection, allowing the word to simply penetrate her being, not only during formal quiet prayer, but all day long. This is her initial active prayer of recollection described earlier and to be used whenever one is not occupied with things of importance. One would

---

11   Kevin G. Culligan, *Toward a Model of Spiritual Direction Based on the Writings of St. John of the Cross and Carl Rogers: An Exploratory Study, Ph.D. diss. Boston University, 1979, 142-143.*
12   Ibid.

be encouraged to turn the heart and mind to God with a simple word or phrase which makes conversation with God more real than the ego-related things people talk to themselves about all day long. Gradually, even the conversation with God becomes a divine gaze between *God the Beloved* and the soul, who share the intimacy of pure love all day long.

Lectio Divina

Lectio Divina is one form of praying with the sacred Word in Scripture. It can be taught to any age group, including teens. This method of utilizing the Scripture comes naturally to some and others prefer to do it with guidance in a group. In it there is opportunity to go over the same passage multiple times until one *rests* on a word or phrase that carries the entire meaning of the passage to the individual. This fourth stage in the process of lectio is called *contemplatio*. It is a significant part of lectio and one that has been ignored in the past. Our current focus on disposing ourselves for contemplation has revived the full practice of lectio, including its final stage, *contemplatio*. A great teacher can set the stage, but no one can lead one into initial contemplation. According to the spiritual classics, It is only arrived at by means of the direct action of God. Such moments of pure prayer need to be treasured and fostered.

The method of Lectio Divina is normally associated with Scripture. However, individuals often use it for any spiritual reading passage. A wealth of meaning is conveyed when we do not rush through passages. In this way the experience of the saints in prayer often becomes ours. We have an attraction for a virtue or way in which these models of our faith integrated Christian values. Our desire becomes to gain some strength for our own spiritual life in union with theirs. This we call 'the communion of saints.' There was no official canonization of saints in the early church. Saint Paul referred to everyone as a potential *saint*. It doesn't just happen without our cooperation. We can look to Teresa for a developmental path by which this miracle of grace can be allowed to happen.

Simplicity

Simplicity, silence and the prayer of active recollection are closely connected in the second dwelling places. Simplicity is important in the quest for union with God because God is simple. We will see as we progress through the dwelling places of *The Interior Castle* how this developmental spiritual process is all about simplicity. Right here it is sufficient to say that a person actively gets rid of whatever obviously clutters up their life. It may not be easy getting rid of things or relationships that do so. It may also be related to one's life commitment to keep certain things or persons close to us, without being attached to them in a way that detracts from union with God. There are people who can handle simplicity on the physical level. They may be generous with material goods to a fault, but they cannot detach from spiritual goods, relationships or even some religious experience. At various transitional stages this may be an impasse.

Simplicity enables one to go to the essence of things so that God's love can continue to beckon all the way to union. Saints are connected at a very deep level of conscious union because their simplicity opens their intellect and all of their faculties to the inspirations of the Holy Spirit. They were thus, ultimately able to penetrate and taste the mysteries of our faith. Seeing how they themselves are overshadowed by the Holy Spirit, they have no difficulty accepting the mysteries of the Christian faith.

The mysteries of the faith known at first obscurely in contemplation are the same mysteries as those learned in theology, heard about in sermons or discussed in faith sharing groups. The humble practice of faith grows during times of darkness. Saint Bonaventure once said that certitude is obtained in the darkness of faith. Humble simplicity also enables one to accept the vast variety of valid religious experience, even though they are not one's own. As we will see in the course of this study, the more simple the experience, the more likely it is of God. Let us repeat: Teresa firmly holds that those who do not believe that God can give many favors to us, will not receive them, since God does not force Himself on anyone. We need to thank God for all of his gifts, especially for the gift of himself in prayer.

Silence

God's first language is silence. This is something to foster in our culture. A group leader in church activities needs to be aware that certain people will resist silence and it will then be the role of the person in charge to provide it for the other members of the group, even though it may be difficult. A few minutes at the end of lectio, after a reading, or following reflections in a prayer service, may be some suggested times for silence. Once aware of the need for it there will be many opportunities to provide silence. An observant spiritual leader will note that there are those who thrive on silence and will thus want to find ways to provide more of it for them.

The temptation may be to always provide recreation or entertainment even on retreats. This needs to be avoided as it can be gotten elsewhere. God whose love beckons, has silence as a first language. Leadership must be encouraged to provide *silence* in order to dispose ordinary Christians for contemplation. There are certain kinds of healing that can only be done at a deeper level of consciousness. This level is arrived at in silence. Attempts to constantly cover up pain with laughter results in no movement. When there is no progress for a long time, a trained spiritual director will opt for a change of some kind. The person needs therapy, a twelve step program or something else.

While the mystical life of grace is generally available to all Christians who believe in it and desire union with God, there may be serious psychological blocks which inhibit the flow of this or any relationship. Is one's fear of silence a basic lack of trust due to childhood neglect or some other trauma? Then this basic lack of trust must be dealt with first. Somehow, tactfully, this person must be guided personally so as not to disrupt the value of silence for everyone else.

Many find silence during the early morning hours before the rest of the world wakes up. Some can successfully build it into another time of day. There is no spiritual growth without it. It must gradually become a time to *rest* in God and not merely do 'our own psychological work.' Self- help activities do belong to the first three dwelling places as one seeks to iron out the incongruous behaviors that exist within a framework of ideal values.

The Prayer of Recollection

The prayer of recollection takes up two chapters in Teresa of Avila's *Way of Perfection*, chapters twenty-eight and twenty–nine. By the time she gets to *The Interior Castle* she sees no need to repeat this material. She sees it as essential from the very beginning. Recollection is something that will just not happen by itself. It must be fostered. It is essential to grow in an awareness of God throughout one's busy day. *Active recollection* is defined as briefly drawing the faculties inward to simply *become aware* of God. The *prayer of simplicity* can also be easily inserted into one's daily *formal* prayer. It is defined as a short phrase or word that calls one back to the presence of God during times of silent personal or group prayer.

Poulan, a Jesuit scholar who valued the contemplative life for all did forty years of research on contemplation. His work is called *The Graces of Interior Prayer*. Initially he focuses on the prayer of active recollection and the prayer of simplicity as is practiced by those doing active ministry. He teaches that it is a monumental mistake to think that there is meditation and then suddenly ecstasy with nothing in between. How many spiritual directors are there who have never heard of the *in between*? He implies that most of them have not. Modern contemplative prayer groups foster the active prayer of recollection although its members do not always recognize its counterpart in the writings of Teresa of Avila. They also follow some form of the prayer of simplicity based on the spiritual classic, *The Cloud of Unknowing*, written by an unknown English mystic of the fourteenth century, although most of them have never read it. In addition to *The Interior Castle*, many of these spiritual classics will be studied by serious spiritual directors.

Poulan gives examples of founders of active communities who thrived by recommending the active prayer of recollection in their formation programs. They quickly noted that their novices were attracted to the prayer of simplicity as a word or two that held them in prayer as well as throughout their day. These very same methods, which are used by lay contemplative communities today, have not often been fostered in all active communities of religious brothers, sisters and diocesan priests. However, some members do stumble upon them, being guided to do so by the Holy Spirit. Today both active and contemplative community members, both lay and religious communities share what they know about prayer with the entire Christian community, with whomever is interested. The laity seem to be taking the lead because in larger numbers they seem to be most willing to learn. There is a great thirst to connect using the prayer of simplicity during times of formal and private quiet prayer.

A member of our contemplative prayer group once questioned how she came to understand the transition from meditation to contemplation when it seemed to her that many of the clergy she asked for help were not sure what to tell her. It was a difficult question and all that came to mind was the gospel story about the master who invited a certain group to his feast and they did not come, so he sent servants out to invite everyone. That seems to be the state of affairs we are happily in. Everyone is invited to union with God. Why else would God have made us, allowing his Son to be our Way back home in the intimacy of Love? We share the same Holy Spirit, Love. It is God's delight that we as humans, of all creatures, can return his love. Mutuality is a most exciting dimension of relationship. It is one of the goals *Love Beckons* has in mind for those who persevere through these dwelling places.

The prayer of recollection underlies all vocal, liturgical and mental prayer. We must try to be aware of the one with whom we are speaking. It is also basic to the prayer of simplicity in which we gradually learn to listen to the one with whom we speak. Once having discovered it, Teresa practiced it for the rest of her life. She knew that since we are not always held in contemplation, we do need to practice recollection often during our busy day. The flow between contemplation and the prayer of recollection is as natural as breathing. A person in the pews, who has learned a set number of memorized prayers as the only way to God is being deprived of an accessible means of conscious union with

God. Teresa valued vocal prayer, especially the *Our Father,* as well as liturgical prayer. She encourages us to look at Jesus to see the Father. She warns us to never get so 'spiritual' that we stop looking at Jesus. The crosses that may come to us in later life and the path to the deepest union with God cannot be endured without the example and presence Jesus.

The Old Testament desire to 'see the face of God' becomes possible in Jesus. *Who sees Me sees My Father* (Jn 14:9). This focus, always looking at the One to whom we pray eventually carries us through our day. For those who have not been taught to enter within and to focus, never usually experience union with God. The prayer of recollection is an essential form of prayer between meditation, discursive prayer and contemplation. Teresa believes we should start teaching the active prayer of recollection here in the second dwelling places.

As has been said, this is simply done. Whenever the mind is free from responsibilities, it is beneficial to turn away from conversation with self and turn toward God. Conversation with God will have more words to it at first and then fewer. It is like any other love relationship and as we will see, is the foundation for all deep love. As we turn from ego conversation with self and reach out in love to others we gradually become concerned about them and forget ourselves. Another stage is to find our deepest self in God. To experience this is eventually to know all things in him.

The Prayer of Simplicity

Studying the ways active communities dispose members for contemplative prayer, Poulan expresses regret that the prayer of simplicity was not always clearly distinguished from mystic prayer, noting that those who did not encourage the prayer of simplicity in their communities did not see growth. He concludes: *It is greatly to be desired that in our days some slight idea, at least, of this degree should be given...*instead of letting it be supposed that there is nothing between meditation and ecstasy. Many directors have never heard of this stage of prayer. How can they then direct the numberless persons who come to this state? [13]

In his careful analysis of discursive prayer Poulan divides it into four stages: vocal prayer, meditation, affective prayer and the prayer of simplicity.[14] His use of the word *ordinary* for meditation, however, can be misleading should people assume that affective prayer and the prayer of simplicity are not ordinary. Thomas Aquinas, Garrigou-Lagrange and other experts on prayer teach that the mystical life is the full development of the life of grace. Only extraordinary phenomena, which is neither to be desired nor rejected, will fall outside this ordinary grace of mystical union.

Extraordinary phenomena, in fact, is extraordinary, not in itself, but because it is not God's ordinary way of operation within, which is entirely beyond the senses and faculties. In other words, when extraordinary phenomena is valid, God descends to the level of our senses and faculties, rather than raising us up to his level of simple union.

For this reason one should desire contemplation, union with God, but not extraordinary phenomena, which is subject to human error and misinterpretation. Later, we will see how Teresa's *intellectual vision* and John of the Cross' *substantial knowledge are described as the essence of valid religious experience*. In these second dwelling places Teresa recommends that beginners not even think of such things as it is a poor way to make a solid foundation for one's prayer life.

The prayer of simplicity is what disposes us to know God is there. This is one revelation God wants to make even more than we want it. Spiritual writers believe it is some form of non-surrender which holds us back. Some lack of trust that God wants what is best for us, God's very self in the union of love. The gift of God is already given. Human longing for it must go beyond feeling. Taking a pilgrimage through the dwelling places enables individuals and spiritual directors to understand the developmental process which makes conscious union with God possible.

---

13   R.P.Poulan, S.j., *The Graces of Interior Prayer* (St. Louis, Mo.:B.Herder, 1910) ,7-51.
14   Ibid.

Indirect Operation of God - Second Dwelling Places

Here God's action, drawing a person into greater light toward the center of the castle, the human soul, is achieved through the words and actions of good people. Words spoken in sermons, written in books and shared with friends are the means to deeper interiority. Illnesses and other setbacks can also be received as a form of grace. Insignts we arrive at during moments of prayer, brief though they be, help us integrate exterior events and interior presence. Teresa does not want us to underestimate these first beginnings of prayer, nor does she want us to become discouraged at our own poor response to God's invitation to love.

His Majesty, as Teresa calls God, who is lord of the castle, our soul, is patient. The exercise of the faculties, the memory, intellect and will, in these dwelling places are the recipients of the indirect operation of the Holy Spirit. One is inspired initially through all the means of human knowledge, which come to the intellect through the senses. In the second dwelling places Teresa encourages us to learn from and converse with persons who will be of some advantage toward growth in deeper spirituality. She will also encourage an active prayer of recollection which will help eliminate the destructive conversation with self which normally goes on in the undisciplined consciousness of persons with no method of control. Finally, Teresa directs us to conversation with God through mental prayer which becomes more and more affective as well as simple, even before the direct action of God takes place in initial contemplation.

Signposts - Second Dwelling Places

The light from the center of the castle is still very slight in the second set of rooms moving slightly toward the place of purest love at the center. One's motivation may be superficial. For example, good works may be done to attract attention. One may resent that others are noticed, even undermining their efforts in ministry. Prayer is still not frequent. There are many distractions and some interior disquiet. Change for the good is difficult and spiritual guidance may not even be desired. Consolations, however, are often sought.

Spiritual Practices - Second Dwelling Places

Courage is needed to listen to God's voice through others. Church leaders can strive to increase prayer times during their activities by fostering personal prayer, liturgical services and lectio divina. Those growing in virtue will learn to accept their faults with humility and may use a gratitude journal, learning to be grateful for what is. The study of Scripture is always recommended and may be used for conversation with Christ. Spiritual conversation ideally replaces self-dialogue of an ego nature.

Teresa reminds us that in these dwelling places it does not rain manna. It is a poor beginning to the spiritual journey to start building it on sand by seeking consolations in prayer or for one's good deeds. Later, when one wants only what God wants, the person will find in the manna every taste one desires and consolation, as it were, everywhere.

Conclusion

The second dwelling places are filled with those willing to learn through classes and conversations from those who model what they wish to arrive at on the spiritual journey. It is a time to replace our self-conversation with spiritual conversation with others and with God. This is a time in which to develop the active prayer of recollection. In the second dwelling places a person ideally fosters the value of silence and recollection in the midst of vocal prayer, meditation and daily life.

3

Solid Food

In the Third dwelling places one has arrived, initially, at an organized life interiorly and exteriorly. Robert was such a well-organized individual both interiorly and exteriorly. In addition, Robert was kind and forgiving. He was a leader and volunteer wherever he might be of service. He attended a long awaited week-end retreat with the men from his church. Although he did not know it at first, Robert was ready to receive God's love, the gift of prayer in a new way.

Robert's Story

All of the men on the retreat were getting a lot out of the talks and discussions. Robert was in what we might call a 'void'. He might have gotten more, he initially thought, by staying home watching one of his favorite movie channels. Robert went to the chapel and buried his head in his hands. He may as well have been burying his entire body and soul for all of the life he had experienced on this retreat. Robert somehow surrendered to the situation and decided to remain for the week-end. He perceived quite vividly that the other men were being filled with the Holy Spirit as on that first Pentecost. Not knowing that his darkness was God's love beckoning to a deeper prayer, Robert remained in total trust in a kind of spiritual dark 'dizziness' described by our spiritual experts as a latent prayer of quiet or the dark night of sense. Many times this state lasts longer than a few days or hours on a retreat. When least expected, a positive result may take place.

And so it was that in an unexpected instant a sensation of warmth flooded Robert. The men filing into the church had living flames over their heads. He could not see the Holy Spirit, hovering above his head. However, from his head down to his toes, Robert was engulfed in what he called 'a molten liquid gold.' Nothing could more graphically describe *an infused grace,* a pouring of God's love into the soul, than Robert's description of this moment. Not only that, but over the years Robert was changed and he knew that there was no going back.

Although he never attended a class on centering prayer so as to dispose himself for contemplation, Robert could close his eyes anywhere and be in prayer. The noisiest places, such as a carnival, where he volunteered for charity, were not off his prayer radar. And Robert always prayed before volunteer work. Very few knew he was praying. It looked like he was resting his eyes or even sleeping.

However, the facilitator of the local contemplative prayer group guessed what he was doing and asked Robert how he could pray with polka music blaring. This music made her want to dance! Robert was dancing alright. It was an interior kind of movement, entirely still and yet, entirely dynamic. Many people of a theological bent call the inner life of God, *the dance of the Father, Son and Holy Spirit,* a communion in Love upon which all love rests. It is both *transcendent* and *immanent.* Both beyond us and very much within us. Robert may not have known this bit of theology. He did enter a bit more closely into that *divine dance* every time he prayed, especially when it was accompanied by polka music!

Dark Night of Sense

When Robert experienced the 'void' at the start of the retreat and throughout it, when nothing worked for him, it was the *dark night of sense.* The presentations, conversations, and reflections on the intellectual level, fed by the senses, no longer gave Robert a sense of satisfaction. Had he left the retreat or given up prayer entirely, Robert would not have made the transition to the next wonderful part of the spiritual journey. This will be discussed in the next chapter on *supernatural prayer* known as *the prayer of quiet*. According to the spiritual doctors of the Church, whose research we will be using, this is the result of God's direct action.

The Night of Sense, at the end of the third dwelling places, is a relatively difficult transition. The person does not know what is happening. It is an entirely new experience and the person's life feels like it is falling apart. Many forms of detachment a person would not even know they need, are experienced. Often the experience of *void* will last longer than Robert's.

A spiritual director with experience in these ways of God is a great help, if the person is to continue to grow through this time of darkness in which the rational intellect does not work on matters of spirituality for personal benefit. In all other ways or even for the spirituality of others, this person may appear brilliant. One wonders during this transition how it is that one can inspire others and not oneself.

We are told that many people arrive here. This transition, however, does not happen without our consent. And there are varying intensities of it. The most difficult sensual trials and temptations are explained in John of the Cross.[15] They are given significant consideration in the dissertation of Kevin Culligan as well as in the writings of Susan Muto.[16] People who experience the most intense *night of sense* are led directly into or are at least destined for *the obscure night of the spirit*.

More often people do not even know they have moved into moments of contemplation. They tend to think they need to be really perfect in order to do so. Many do not realize that contemplation is what gradually makes one more perfect. God's direct action is better at perfecting people than human effort is. Often there is no consciousness of the *crud* needing removal from the beautiful crystal castle of the soul, so that the radiant light within can shine forth.

---

15 John of the Cross, *The Dark Night, Book One* , *chapter fourteen* in The Collected Works of St. John of the Cross, Kavanaugh, (Washington D.C.: ICS, 1991), 392-394.

16 Culligan, diss., 297.
     See also: Susan Muto, *John of the Cross for Today* (Pittsburgh: Epiphany Association, 2000),141-152.

After some time of actively practicing the faith, there sets in a disenchantment with it all. The well- organized life at the end of the third dwelling places does not reward one with a feeling of satisfaction. Rather, if one is truly humble, this transition feels like one is going backwards. Teresa tells us that if a person is humble, this is a most excellent state, but without humility one will stay here the rest of one's life with a thousand afflictions and miseries.[17] It is amazing and the cliché seems to be true here, "When the student is ready, the teacher appears."

If a director who understands the dark nights is not available, it may happen that a person discovers the perfect passage in a book. At any time one can pick up a passage on spiritual darkness or some other topic rarely discussed and it can be of great help to them. This is especially true if they cannot find an experienced spiritual director. Clearly, this is the advantage and awesome power of the Word, speaking to us in many forms, including that of the printed page. When the time comes and spiritual director is available, persons cherish very much those who walk with them in dark times. A stable spiritual bond is formed and one would wish for nothing better than to walk with another who endures the experience of spiritual darkness.

Poulan, *Graces of Interior Prayer,* states that a person in the *night of sense* is 'out to sea' and all alone. He is lost and cannot manage the boat. Poulan suggests concrete teaching by an experienced guide for this most important stage on the spiritual journey. "A book or a clear sighted director leads them to moderate their excesses, to reserve a larger share of activity for their spiritual life and not to fly from their inward purgatory."[18] It is not suggested that one experiencing this transition be guided by an indirect method. Since it will not work they will go from relationship to relationship, trying to find an answer to their inability to pray. Indirect spiritual direction throws back the discovery of what to do on the directee. Without a wealth of resources, a person would never imagine what is going on here. This understanding might

---

17   Kavanaugh, Castle, 63.
18   Poulan, ibid., 206

take a lifetime of study. Humbly following simple directives from an experienced guide works best. Otherwise one might be tempted to go from one director to another or to give up the spiritual life altogether. The advice of Teresa is to discern carefully when deciding on a spiritual director. The qualities of knowledge and personal experience are to be sought in a director. She puts knowledge as the primary consideration.

The persona, the outer personality, is undergoing a radical change from the inside out. It feels to the person like their soul is contained in a fragile vase. A crack or two can be repaired, but now it feels like the entire vase has been shattered. One is devastated. The scene looks like that after a severe natural disaster. Nothing recognizable is left on the spiritual scene. Doing one's own work with the help of therapy alone is not sufficient *in the dark night.* Enlightened therpists today admit the need for a transcendent dimension, which includes spiritual direction. They realize at this time of transition that the major work is an action of the Holy Spirit within. The masks from the false self are shattered and self-help techniques which try to put them back together and back on no longer work.

Pastoral counselors are often not trained in the level of spiritual direction required for this transition. Most spiritual directors require a separate set of instructions for directing contemplatives. The current model, should, but often does not, train spiritual directors to deal with the ongoing development of the Christian mystical life. If Christians are to become conscious of their life within, this will become necessary in the near future.

If the trials and temptations enumerated by John of the Cross are intense enough, a person can learn to hold on at a deeper level. That is the level of contemplation. This is the place of transition where the work becomes God's and one learns to respond to God's direction from within. It is a moment of awakening and becomes a new pattern of life. Through the inflowing of God within the plain food of the *manna in the desert* becomes most satisfying. Eventually, it is preferred to former sense satisfactions.

Many spiritual writers say that one discovers their 'true self' in the process at the end of the third dwelling places. It is that self which is capable of union with God. It is the self, returning to the garden where

Adam and Eve walked together in communion with God and each other. Human longing is now satisfied because it is on the right path, receiving God's gift of love and sharing it in spiritual communion with others.

What One Brings to the Third Dwelling Places

A person brings a lot of ego motivation to the third dwelling places. The many self-help skills provided by psychology are the materials used even by spiritual directors in the first three dwelling places. It is the purpose of the dark night of sense to transition one into contemplative prayer. Some might put this transition between the third and fourth dwelling places. It seems to me that Teresa puts it at the end of the third dwelling places because it is here that she refers to spiritual dryness. She admonishes us not to put too much store in it because there are others who have many more intense trials.[19] All of this speaks of the degrees of intensity taught by John of the Cross and studied by spiritual directors for contemplatives.

Teresa knows that the trials at the end of the third dwelling places would be forgotten in the experience of God's love as soon as contemplative prayer sets in. Therefore, she seemed to leave this difficult state to John of the Cross, who spends much time explaining it. The outcome of the dark night correctly understood and accepted is expressed in a mystical understanding of the book of Revelation, "All tears will be wiped from their eyes. They will look upon his face, and his name will be written on their foreheads. Night will be no more, nor will they need light from lamp or sun, for the Lord God shall give them light, and they shall reign forever and ever."[20]

The fact that the beginning of the third dwelling places is so different from its final stages is an example of what Teresa means when she says each of the dwelling places has many rooms. *Even millions,* would be the exact translation. This will become clear as we move on and see how different the spiritual awakenings and experiences of individuals can be. A spiritual director must hold them lightly, not making

---

19   Kavanaugh, Castle, 58
20   Rev: 21:4; 22:4-5.

too much or too little of them. As the envoy of the Holy Spirit, the Consoler, one learns to respect God's way of acting with each and to value experiences that are not one's own, provided they are humble experiences.

A friend once warned me that getting into this field might open a director up to a few people with mental problems. Quite the opposite is true. However, it is a good idea to know one such type of individual just to note the difference between a person who 'flaunts' it and one who holds every gift of God, especially God's own gift of Self, with great humility. It is rather easy to tell the difference.

Divine Operation in the Night of Sense

In book one, chapter eight of *The Dark Night* John of the Cross sets forth the purpose of the night of sense as the purification of the senses in order to accommodate them to the spirit. *The sensory night is common and happens to many. These are the beginners whom we will treat first.*[21]

John of the Cross explains that initially these beginners, through meditation and the practice of virtues, have been able to turn away from worldly things and have gained strength in God to go on in dryness, while suffering a little oppression and without turning back. Since their love of God is still not too distant from their love of pleasure and self, God wishes to lead beyond this base manner of loving. In order to do so, he desires to lead them to a higher degree of love.

> *And he desires to liberate them from the lowly exercise of the senses and of discursive meditation, by which they go in search of him so inadequately and with so many difficulties, and lead them into the exercise of spirit, in which they become capable of a communion with God that is more abundant and more free of imperfections... This usually happens to recollected beginners sooner than to others since they are freer from occasions of backsliding... A reform of the desires is the*

---

21   St. John of the Cross, *Collected Works of St. John of the Cross*, Kavanaugh K, O.C.D. and Rodriquez,O., O.C.D.trans.(Washington D.C.: ICS, 1991), 375.

requirement for entering the happy night of sense. Not much time or-
dinarily passes after the initial stages of their spiritual life before begin-
ners start to enter the night of sense... It is common to see them suffer
these aridities.[22]

Both Teresa and John of the Cross compare the solid food of this
stage to the manna provided by God as heavenly food. It is at first un-
desirable to a palate which is used to more satisfying, but less substantial food. Now, however, there is an inclination to remain silent in spite
of the fact that nothing satisfying seems to be going on in prayer. This
is due to the fact that the rational intellect is not being fed through the
senses. One is being fed, but on a deeper level than one is familiar with.
When the transition to mystical prayer is permanent, interior nourish-
ment will be received as a kind of holy idleness in prayer.

It is true, though, that at times in the beginning the purgation of some
souls is not continuous in such a way that they are always deprived
of sensory satisfaction and the ability to meditate... Nevertheless, if
they are to advance... they will leave further behind the work of their
senses.[23]

For this reason many do not recognize in themselves or their directees the full force of this transition described in John of the Cross. In his
poem *The Dark Night*, John of the Cross tells us that he escaped not
only from his captors, who held him in prison, but, he fled most essentially from his own senses and faculties, which held him in spiritual
bondage. He recalls that he was not seen by his guards as he escaped.
Nor were his senses able to tell how it was that his interior house was
now at rest. The divine operation in contemplation is unknown to the
human senses and faculties. The soul states that it was able to make
this escape because of the strength and warmth gained from loving
its Bridegroom in this obscure contemplation. The soul delights in its

22 Ibid., 376 -377.
23 Ibid., 380.

success because none of its enemies: the world, the flesh and the devil can impede it in this night of purifying contemplation. Lulled to sleep are all the selfish attachments, movements and passions which abide in one's house of sense. One hears people instill fear in others of any kind of silence as a place evil can attack. John of the Cross tells us the opposite. It is here, in the safety of the divine operation of uncreated love, that one is safe. One is going out into the safety of God's love.

Poulan makes a powerful observation, describing *The Night of Sense* as a latent *Prayer of Quiet*. He observes that before John of the Cross people did not at all value the dryness of this stage as anything significant. They did not see the direct action of God in it.[24] These days the 'void' experienced in *The Night of Sense* is often confused with depression. Because it is out of a psychologist's field to deal with contemplation, a person can be side-tracked for a long time. There is a vast difference between a 'void' that is supernatural and is intended to be filled with God and one that is the dead-end to personality. My experience is that certain medications can cause depression, especially end-stage cancer medications. Even persons who previously worked their way through *The Dark Night of Sense* and were well on their way in the practice of contemplative prayer may experience the effects of medications.

The spiritual director who understands the importance of this transition to contemplation will find it difficult to communicate it to their suffering directee, but must try at all costs to keep them faithful to prayer. In this way, after a latent stage of contemplation in the dark night of sense is followed by the prayer of quiet, one will begin to value the work of love God has begun in them. It is not something to be taken lightly.

The Likeness of Love

Teresa of Avila advocates spiritual friendships for a good reason. We must be careful who our friends are because *the likeness of love* pushes out all that is not in tune with it. 'Friendship with Jesus' and 'Friendship with God' are often topics of spiritual talks. Here the

---

24   Poulan, Ibid., 207-210.

likeness of God's love gradually pushes out all that is not consistent with it. We become like that which we love. If it is true that *God is Love* in our world view, then we want to rid ourselves of all that is not God. Only The Holy Spirit can complete the project for us. This wonderful work of grace is begun in *the night of sense.* The rational mind which acquires its concepts through the senses is not capable of so great a love. To grow in this consciousness of pure love requires the darkness of *The Night of Sense.* John of the Cross tells us that this stage is more of an accommodation of the senses to the spirit than it is a real purgation. When one understands its most intense form, leading directly to *the night of spirit,* this is understandable.

Accommodation of the senses to the spirit is necessary for union with God in initial contemplation. *The dark night of sense* is really an accommodation and not a purgation. St. Paul tells us that one is united to God when it is a Spirit to spirit union. The dark night prepares us for such a union. It seems to me that *the night of sense* is a passage from reliance on the rational intellect to reliance on the intuitive intellect. Later, the entire intellect will undergo a passive purgation. The human spirit and the divine Spirit will become one in love. This is pure love is a consciousness of who we are meant to be. Many have come to think of the *true self* as the receptive self. This self is opposed to the persona, operating out of what is expected by others rather than with the integrity of who one really is.

Signposts - Third Dwelling Places

Experiencing a well ordered life on every level may very well foster pride in the beginning third dwelling places. Temptations and dryness may indicate to an experienced director that a positive transition is taking place. Former methods no longer work. It bears repeating that one feels lost at sea until someone with experience of this vital transition explains the significance of the **void** which precedes initial contemplation. Where directors are not available, sometimes a book will help. However, the vast number of people are not exposed to spiritual writings of this caliber and so this precious moment can be lost at sea forever.

This is a great loss, not only for the person, but for humanity. The spiritual doctors of the church tell us that many arrive at this transition, but few pass beyond it. Realizing the importance of one's entry into contemplation, Teresa of Avila prays fervently, not only to understand it, but for the words to explain it. She sees each of these as valuable, but separate gifts given for the good of others.

Spiritual Practices - Third Dwelling Places

During *the dark night of sense* spiritual direction is not a luxury, but a necessity. The person experiencing temptations, sometimes of a violent nature, must be reminded to go on in faith to a place deeper within than the place in which the temptations occur. It is recommended to hold on in faith and to offer these trials for people who really do desire the evil represented in these outpourings of the unconscious. These buried or repressed contents of the unconscious make themselves slightly felt at first. Later in the liberation afforded by *the dark night of the spirit* we will consider the complete *outpouring of the unconscious*. It is for this reason that the dark night can be defined as *a change of consciousness*.

A person learns to accept the trials and dryness of this stage in peace, even if they think this condition could last forever. One does not see a way out. This possibility of it lasting forever seems very real at the time. Reading an author with some understanding of this stage is a great help. It provides an objective norm to cling to. The author does not even know the person reading this and yet explains their interior state quite well. And so a person can conclude that this must be a significant part of the Christian journey. To find oneself in the Christian community of faith, even in one's interior experience, is essential. Spiritual reading about experiences that are like our own become an invaluable resource. The stories of real individuals, most of whom are alive today, may assist readers in locating their own experience as valuable in the Christian community of today. It is crucial to remember that only certain things we find in spiritual reading will be an attraction of grace for us. This is the Holy Spirit acting through the

Word which carries a special grace for us. We do not travel the entire journey inward in one reading. It may take years and even a lifetime. Your time has been a success if you gain one pertinent idea from a chapter or even from the entire book. The significance of your shared Christian experience with another will be the intensity with which it draws you to union with God. For this reason Teresa of Avila valued spiritual friendship as a significant grace not to be taken lightly.

While one may prefer a simple form of prayer at any time as long as this person stays close to Christian Scripture, to adopt a form of the 'prayer of simplicity' is essential when nothing else works. The pattern of growth is: meditation, affective prayer, prayer of simplicity and contemplation. The spiritual classic *The Cloud of Unknowing* by an unknown English mystic explains the value of a sacred word as one form of the prayer of simplicity. Since one is not always held in contemplation, especially in the beginning, it is important to know what to do in the meantime. Teresa always had an inspiring book handy for such times. One often prefers a line or word or even just a breath to begin prayer. These could all be considered the 'prayer of simplicity'. Some people, just by sitting in their chair with a good posture, find it enough to enter into the stillness of God.

One should be encouraged to realize that the fullness of union with God is something to be desired. Thomas Merton once said that God gives the desire before the gift. Teresa saw no reason why those who desire it should not be given entrance into the final dwelling places of the most complete union with God even in this life. Desire, human longing for this union, is in the mind of Teresa an excellent preparation for it. We must not desire a phenomenal experience such as Robert had in this story. It cannot be repeated often enough that we are to be encouraged to seek only union with God. The Holy Spirit desires this union with us even more. It is the purpose of the Incarnation and the life of Jesus on this earth. How can we miss this point and think it is only for a rare few?

We tend to listen to well-known people. It seems that certain brilliant teachers promoted the idea that the mystical life is about extraordinary phenomenal experiences and therefore, it is the lot of only a few.

Since we have learned this position over the years some have concluded that union with God is exceptional. Nothing could be farther from the truth.

Directors must hold lightly the valid experiences of all who come to them. If it is phenomenal and accepted in humility, that is fine. If there are no phenomenal or extraordinary experiences, that is fine, too. These are not the essence of union with God. It could be the length of the sixth dwelling places which has convinced the inexperienced that phenomenal experience is important. This is not even the most significant topic in the sixth dwelling places. Since extraordinary experience was a problem in sixteenth century Spain it is covered in great detail. Teresa reminds us that especially in the beginning one should not be concerned about such things. Here one is encouraged to accept the ordinary dryness that accompanies the night of sense at the end of the third dwelling places. Teresa reminds us not to make too much of dryness. It is slight in comparison with the trials that others face.

Signposts - Dark Night of Sense

Since spiritual directors are called upon to witness to the transition from meditation to contemplation, to know the three signs of this transition is absolutely necessary. Poulan sets forth a chapter on 'interrogation' in which he instructs directors on how to discern if directees are entering the contemplative way permanently. Most of the time the initial moments of contemplation alternate with moments when one can meditate on Scripture, pray vocally and enter with ease into the prayer life of the community. Therefore, most of us will find these three simple signposts sufficient:

1. When one is entering the dark night of sense one cannot pray or meditate in the accustomed manner.
2. There is a lack of satisfaction with spiritual things and with life in general.
3. Most significantly, there is a desire to be alone with God though nothing seems to be happening. Nothing is everything.

Since the inability to pray or the lack of satisfaction can have other causes, the ultimately significant sign of a call to contemplation is the third one. When all three are taken together for some time, a spiritual director can safely guide a person to the prayer of simplicity in any form which suits the person. This will dispose the person for contemplation as the Holy Spirit sees fit. To the extent that it is possible and required by one's state in life, one should enter into the prayer of the community. Although one cannot pray or work in a way that formerly brought satisfaction, one is usually quite excellent in the work performed. No one but the person involved and their director may know the difficulty going on. If the person writes or gives talks in some form of ministry, they will wonder how they can inspire so many others. There seems to be no source of inspiration on their personal horizon.

Most significantly, the person transitioning to contemplation will eventually desire to be alone with God in emptiness, poverty and spiritual nakedness. This is most significant because a mere lack of satisfaction can be caused by health issues, depression or other circumstances in life. The faithfulness in prayer with a desire for God alone, especially when there is no satisfaction in it, is crucial. The person shows up for silent prayer because God deserves it, not for satisfaction. It is normal to feel like one is going backwards. To begin understanding this gift of grace spiritual direction is absolutely necessary. A person is too close to the emptiness experienced to be able to find any good in it on their own.

Spiritual Practices - Dark Night of Sense

Staying faithful to a simple focus on prayer when nothing seems to be happening is the major spiritual practice required in the night of sense. One centers their will on God in the prayer of simplicity by *showing up for prayer on a regular basis.* There is no desire for control with regard to how the time in prayer will go. Gradually, one sees this detachment applied to the outcome of events in daily life. Others notice the person is more peaceful. Selfish clinging to persons, places and things is significantly reduced. The intuitive intellect becomes predominant, replacing the rational intellect in regard to spiritual matters. One relies on symbols to explain the deep interior movement of the Holy Spirit. It is easier to arrive at the *essence* of things.

Benefits of the Dark Night of Sense

A person is liberated from much misery which is encountered as one sense desire replaces another. For these do not satisfy. The distaste in spiritual exercises dries up lust, both sensual and spiritual. There is no longer a greediness for an abundance of religious objects or to complete many devotions. Abiding within, is a desire to love and please God alone. One is gradually more conscious of God's presence throughout the day. The fruits of the Holy Spirit are given with every virtue strengthened. Having been freed of selfish desires, one proceeds in peace. Peace is no small gift. It is the fruit of the Holy Spirit which most marks a successful passage in this stage of transition. As I have previously indicated, when discerning the events of life, it is second nature for the person who has made this transition to distinguish the essential from the non-essential. Finally, St. John of the Cross tells us that when least expected God communicates moments of delicate contemplation with spiritual sweetness and knowledge.

Conclusion

The divine operation at the end of the third dwelling places eventually convinces one that the work done by the Holy Spirit is essential for union with God. We have come to the place where we can admit that we cannot perfect ourselves. The impasse experienced in these dwelling places feels monumental. Things are falling apart with no apparent reason. A person without experience of the interior life is beside themselves. As has been mentioned earlier, it is here that even the most non-directive spiritual guide must admit the absolute need for direct teaching related to the importance of this interior transition. At times even those trained in teaching an introductory program for contemplative prayer do not recognize contempation when they see it. It is important to value beyond our own teaching the subtle transition to contemplation, which is extremely delicate. This is a painful place to be all alone and without guidance. It is easy to turn back and give up the spiritual life entirely. Dealing with the interior experience is more crucial than a choice of lifestyle. There are many who reach this place without proper direction. The temptation is to keep trying different things. Since the transition to deeper prayer is within, changing only exterior things does not work. Many find that therapy does not work. Nor does trying a new spiritual book or religion. Some may conclude that God is just not there for them. One must learn to sit still in order to learn just how much God will make himself known for them. Teresa tells us that God's gift of love is leading to a deep union through supernatural prayer, which has not been experienced by the person previously. The direct action of God known as *the prayer of quiet* is the first touch of mystical union presented by Teresa of Avila in *The Interior Castle*. We will take up this and the initial prayer of *infused recollection* in the fourth dwelling places. We pray that The Holy Spirit allows these pages to reach those searching for this deeper, direct union with God.

4

Bathed in Love

At the end of chapter three we saw how perseverance is needed in times of dryness, when nothing seems to be working in one's spiritual life. We have seen as well how this might indicate the divine operation as a preparation in the dark night of sense for the prayer of quiet, generally considered the entry into contemplation.

Luke's Story

The story of Luke is one of quiet supernatural prayer. Luke never had any phenomenal or extraordinary religious experience. Yet, outside of his contemplative prayer group, he was thought of as a mystic. After a time of struggle in silent prayer, both Luke and a friend of his in the group each reported an experience of ease with quiet prayer when it was least expected. Their descriptions sounded very much like the *prayer of quiet* to be discussed in this fourth chapter. A wise woman in the group spoke up and told the men that of course, they would not be able to do this whenever they wished. It was the gift of God.

Luke and his friend understood the meaning of these words as they individually experienced the prayer of quiet for the first time. Luke never spoke of it again. He had a penchant for teaching the class. He would stand up and expound on what he discovered during the course of the week in studying John of the Cross. Luke loved to compare the writings of John of the Cross to Mother Therese of Calcutta and to the writings of Thomas Merton. He always wished that the contemplative prayer group would grow in numbers. The facilitator was pleased with the smaller number because the depth of each person was amazing to her. Many in the local congregation did not understand this type of prayer, but had to recognize that the ministry of this group in serving the sick was extraordinary. Luke, for example, brought Holy Communion to the mentally ill. The woman who instructed him on the nature of the prayer of quiet had her most significant prayer experiences while being a Communion minister to the elderly. Although she found them drooling and even insulting at times, the moments with them were the sweetest prayer she had known. This reminded the facilitator of the closing line in Teresa of Avila's *Interior Castle,* where she is speaking of the mystical marriage. "*The purpose of this marriage is good works.*" Teresa told her cloistered sisters, if there were a sick lady down the street, they should leave their prayer and go to minister to her.

We can only imagine that anyone who saw Luke as a mystic did so because of his extraordinary kindness, his non-judgmental attitude and his willingness to serve by teaching. He brought in helpful materials related to Christian contemplation and took care to provide excellent presentations. Having spent time with many centering prayer groups as well as many sessions in Christian Meditation, it would be hard to come upon a member as well versed in the Christian mystical life. And as Teresa valued it in her own case, Luke also had the ability to impart it. To the members of the group Luke seemed no different than any of them. All enjoyed his sharing with them as well as the lively discussions that followed. They shared his love for the elderly, sick and poor of the community. Like Luke, many in this group had a ministry of some sort with those most in need.

The third dwelling places mark the stage of the mature Christian who has arrived as far as pssible by means of personal effort at a self-less attitude. Through the faithful reception of the sacraments and meditation on the life of Christ in Scripture, the mature Christian actively seeks to conform his life to Christ. One does this through the practice of the virtues as well as through the acceptance of the many challenges faced in the course of life. These efforts are defined by John of the Cross as the active night of sense. Here, in the fourth dwelling places, one has already encountered the experience of the passive night of sense. It is this element which needs to be discerned by a spiritual director before a directee formally enters a life centered on contemplative prayer. And so with the signs of no comfort in the things of God or in anything else, as well as the feeling of going backward in the spiritual life with a solicitude for the things of God, a spiritual director may look for the third and most important sign to discern if this person likes to be alone with God though nothing seems to be happening.[25]

The director recognizes that it is the Holy Spirit holding the will of the person in prayer. At first in the prayer of quiet, it may be for very short moments. Now the Holy Spirit is gradually transforming the will to desire Love alone, a love worthy of complete union with God. The person may return to discursive prayer intermittently, but will learn how to respond with sensitivity to God's direct touch. One will need to recognize the operation of uncreated grace calling people to this deeper prayer of quiet. The movement of grace is so subtle at first that it is often ignored. When it is clearly experienced, most often the *prayer of quiet* is recognized as the first prayer of contemplation. Teresa treats of it first in the fourth dwelling places. However, she herself, speaks of an even more delicate and primary prayer called the prayer of (infused) recollection. She and John of the Cross compare this prayer to the shepherd's whistle. Only the sheep hear and recognize the call of their shepherd. So delicate is this call that it can hardly be identified. This recollection is different from the active recollection Teresa advises in the first three dwelling places and beyond. It comes upon one when

---

25   Culligan, diss., 289-292.
      See also: *Clinical Depression and the Dark Night in Presence* (Spiritual Directors' International Publication, vol. 19 Feb, 2004), 8-19.
      or
      Clinical Depression and the Dark Night on Cassette (Washington D. C.: ICS) #148-5.

saying vocal prayers or when passing one's prayer place or simply for no reason at all. It draws one silently inward. When a little more powerful, one can think of it as a wind tunnel. It is not something one would want to ignore once there is an understanding of what it is.

Both the *prayer of infused recollection* and t*he prayer of quiet* are contemplation in the strict classical sense of the word. Teresa values them so highly that she prays to the Holy Spirit intensely before writing this, just as she does at the beginning of *The Interior Castle.* Teresa realizes it is one thing to experience these things and it is still another to be able to explain them. When she writes of recollection in the fourth dwelling places, she assumes her readers have read and know all about the prayer of active recollection from chapters twenty-eight and twenty-nine in her *Way of Perfection.* This practice is one of turning to God throughout the day whenever free to do so. In the fourth dwelling places Teresa speaks of another kind of recollection in which the Holy Spirit gently draws the soul inward, into what is called *infused recollection.* This gift of grace often precedes *the prayer of quiet.*

The transformative power of contemplation goes far beyond what we ourselves can do. Without contemplation much of the ministry of the church remains social work at best or a flaunting of our own personal gifts. Contemplation is essential for ministry. Those in the ministry of social reformation have recognized this fact because their outreach can be so difficult. The point must come when the work is not our own, but God's. The loving knowledge of contemplation is initiated through an experience of interior darkness, but continues on in the delight of love and the performance of works beyond the scope of human initiative.

The loving sweetness of contemplation is not to be clung to, but it should be treasured when given and is far different from discursive satisfaction, which is a satisfaction with our own job well done. To cling to moments of contemplation is to lose them. It would be something like clinging to a handful of sand. When you wrap your fingers around the sand clinging to it, it pours out through the fingers and is lost. Contemplation is a pure gift of God's love. It is the love for which human kind was created and for which we long. It is such a significant gift of God that there is no cost too great while alerting people to become aware of it.

In the introduction to the fourth dwelling places of *The Interior Castle* translated by E. A. Peers it says:

Here the supernatural element of the mystical life first enters. That is to say, it is no longer by its own efforts that the soul is acquiring what it gains…Hence forward, the soul's part will become increasingly less and God's part increasingly greater. The graces of the fourth mansions… are identified with The Prayer of Quiet, or the Second Water in the *Life*.[26]

Watering the Human Soul with Living Water

Again, Teresa assumes in writing *The Interior Castle* that one knows her analogy of *the four ways of watering the garden*, the human soul. She says that *The Prayer of Quiet* is the second water.

Growing up, Teresa had in her home a picture of Jesus with the woman at the well, a depiction of the gospel story in John, chapter four. It was this image that inspired her to explain the stages of prayer as similar to four ways of watering a garden. These stages of prayer are explained in her Autobiography:

The beginner must think of himself as one setting out to make a garden in which the Lord is to take His delight… It seems to me that the garden can be watered in four ways: by taking water from a well, (meditation) which costs us great labor; by a waterwheel and buckets, (prayer of quiet) which is less laborious and gives more water; by a stream or brook, (prayer of union)which waters the ground much better for it saturates it more thoroughly…and by heavy rain, (transforming union, known as mystical marriage) when the Lord waters it with no labor of ours, a way incomparably better than any of those that have been described.[27]

---

26   E. A. Peers, *The Interior Castle*, (USA : Doubleday, Image, 2000), introduction, xv.
27   St. Teresa of Avila, *The Life of Teresa of Jesus: The Autobiography of Teresa of Avila*, ed. And trans. E.A.Peers (USA: Doubleday, Image, 2004) 75.

Divine Operation in the Fourth Dwelling Places

Describing the prayer of quiet, which corresponds to the second way of watering the garden, the Holy Spirit, as the loving action of God within, holds the will momentarily. That is to say, the will alone is captivated by the living light that manifests the sweet presence of God and his goodness in us. It is like the springing up of the living water which Jesus spoke of to the woman at the well in the fourth chapter of the Gospel of John. The living water springing up from wthin may give a different impression than infused, which means God is poured into the soul. While God is experienced as *immanent,* or indwelling, God is also *transcendent,* or objectively beyond us. Therefore, spiritual maters have most often used the word 'infused' to explain the gift of God in contemplation. Some may prefer to say this love of God found in one's deepest core is *diffused.* However one explains it, this divine action is not up to us.

We experience the greatest peace, calm and sweetness in the inmost depths of our being as the whole physical part of our nature shares in this delight and sweetness. However, in this state the intellect, the memory and the imagination are not yet captivated by the divine action. Sometimes they are the auxiliaries of the will and are occupied in its service; at other times their lack of coopcration serves only to trouble it. Then, according to Teresa, one should pay no attention to them. She compares these faculties to the noisy people in the house of the soul.

The sweet quiet is, in the first stages of contemplative prayer not continual and one cannot, should not, try to produce it. It can be thought of as a gift from the Beloved, which one does not seek. It is the relationship with the Beloved which is sought. All other gifts are appreciated, but not sought. When the relationship with God is no longer primary, all is lost.

The sweetness of the prayer of quiet needs to be appreciated, when it is given, above and beyond any methods taught involving the prayer of simplicity. To disdain the prayer of quiet because one holds rigidly to a mcthod taught is a disaster. Members in contemplative prayer groups need to be instructed as to why they are taught the prayer of simplicity. No method is an end in itself. John of the Cross never taught a method or talked about his own method of prayer. Teresa of Avila uses the method of the prayer of simplicity with great flexibility, according to the needs of the individual. According to William Johnston, the prayer of simplicity can be sought anytime one wishes, provided they stay close to Christian Scripture and have spent some time, usually a few years in meditation and affective prayer. A sensitivity to God's action within is necessary. People have been known to continue forcing themselves into a prayer they have already grown out of. It is as painful as forcing feet into a pair of shoes that are too small. When this happens one can give up prayer altogether. It is a sad state of affairs. For this reason it is good to know something about the developmental stages of prayer as Teresa teaches them.

Understanding Contemplation in Formation

A woman who was quite a philosopher appeared on a talk show and told her story. She was in a novitiate and did her best to say all the prayers required, seeking to practice meditation faithfully. God did not seem to speak to her heart. She thought the life was not for her. She gave up not only this vocation, but her faith as well. She wanted to do a work of transcendence and gives talks on 'spirituality' of a non-religious nature. Had the person in charge of novices seen that this woman's prayer life was in a meaningful transition toward a deeper personal relationship with God, one wonders what heights or depths of union with God this woman would have reached and shared with others.

It is essential for those who train others in prayer to understand contemplation. It is an interior mystical action of God within that beckons persons in every Christian lifestyle, as the stories in this book will continue to show. However, many graces of prayer are lost because a person may have no one available who can assure them concerning what is happening to them. The light from the center of the castle gets stronger as one nears the center. Detachment will become necessary, says Teresa, lest we fail by not disposing ourselves to turn away from all that can hinder this light. Christians of every sort of tradition agree that Teresa of Avila is the one to follow in such matters. She tells us of the delicate power of the Shepherd's whistle, a symbol both she and John of the Cross use for explaining infused recollection:

> *So powerful is this shepherd's call that they give up the things outside the castle which had led them astray…These people are sometimes in the castle before having begun to think about God at all. I cannot say where they entered it or how they heard their Shepherd's call. It was not with their ears, for outwardly such a call is not audible.*[28]

Teresa goes on to explain this interiority of gradually retiring within oneself is something like a turtle withdrawing into its shell. Whoever experiences this will understand what she means. For directors or companions in prayer to insist that persons in their group follow a certain method when they are experiencing the prayer of quiet or moments of infused recollection is dangerous. *Directors can do much harm if they do not know God's ways of leading souls from the lowest and most exterior to the highest and most interior.*[29]

Transient Experience

As a person first experiences initial contemplation there is a need for reassurance that one's will is held in love by the Holy Spirit during the prayer. What arises from the sensory part is to be ignored. The intention is simply to keep one's will in God. These moments of *the prayer of quiet* are common and many experience them. Though short in duration of time, this union with God is significantly effective in the life of the person, producing peace and virtue often noticed by family and friends.

The love of God touches the heart, described by Teresa as a very deep place in the center of the soul, where the secret things of God are learned. *God's love fills the soul not in a noisy way, through pipes, as the water of meditation does, but through a trough that is filled quietly and continually when it is built near its Source.*[30] It will take time for one to

---

28   Peers, Castle, ibid., 69-70.
29   Kavanaugh, *Collected Works of John of the Cross*, 775.
30   Kavanaugh, Castle, 69, 74-75.

become conscious of this secret work of God in the soul. At first the times when the Holy Spirit holds the will are rare moments, but gradually they may increase as one is faithful to prayer. Initially the conscious experience of this operation of divine grace is intermittent.

Another transient experience which occurs in the fourth dwelling places is called the *dilation of the heart* by Teresa. This can be experienced in prayer or during ministry. In it one is powerfully aware that one's heart is filled with God's love, enabling one to spend fruitful time in adoration or in a difficult ministry. The *dilation of the heart* enables a person, full of joy, to minister to the most neglected of humanity.

Teresa encourages us to accept with gratitude these first graces of contemplation:

> *Anyone who is conscious that this is happening within himself should give God great praise, for he will be very right to recognize what a favor it is; and the thanksgiving which he makes for it will prepare him for greater favors (of union in love).[31]*

Continuing to instruct us on this matter, Teresa says that unless the Lord gives absorption in God through contemplation, in which we are much better instructed than through our own efforts, we cannot cease thinking in any way which will not bring us more harm than profit. And so she insists that this prayer be gentle and not forced. It is not possible in our life of exile to live in a state of constant contemplation and absorption in God.[32] Seen in the whole of *The Interior Castle* one comes to realize that contemplation becomes integrated, allowing one to function in a completely normal way. In other words, the will and faculties are not held, in the final stage of the spiritual journey so as to impede action. In the meantime, the experienced director needs to understand just how, not only the will, but the intellect and memory are held in love by the Holy Spirit. In the transformation of the human faculties one is prepared for the most effective ministry. This will be the topic of the fifth and sixth dwelling places.

---

31   Peers, Castle, 70-71.
32   Ibid.

Signposts - Fourth Dwelling Places

Here the spiritual director is called upon to recognize and to witness to the supernatural element in the mystical life. Classical writers define this as God's direct action in the soul, which becomes increasingly greater. Contemplation is most easily recognized at first as a break in vocal prayer. It is an impediment to saying and *doing* discursive prayer. Contemplation becomes *being* in love. Difficulty in completing vocal prayers will be a problem only slightly noticed in the fourth dwelling places. Outside of required prayers, there will be a growing desire to remain alone in loving attention. Once a person understands that there are two forms of the prayer of quiet, it will not matter to them if they experience the dry or the sweet form of initial contemplation. In either case the will is held in loving attention.

Spiritual Practices - Fourth Dwelling Places

Catholic/Christian action, in order to be much more than mere social work, depends on attentiveness to the divine presence and action within. The dilation of the heart, which takes place in the fourth dwelling places, enables one to move to a selfless, even heroic action for the good of others, especially their spiritual good. Therefore, sensitivity to the action of God within must be allowed for and encouraged. One must be encouraged to treasure, but not try to produce contemplation. One must also be instructed to read Scripture and perform devotional practices when possible. After brief moments in the initial *prayer of quiet* it is relatively easy to return to vocal prayer.

Conclusion

The first experience of contemplation as it appears in its latent stage, the night of sense, is not easily recognized by spiritual directors. It is even less easily recognized by the one experiencing it. Factors that may look like the night of sense such as illness or psychological depression can be ruled out when a person longs to be alone with God though nothing seems to be happening.

What classical writers call the direct action of God in contemplation is a most precious gift for an individual and those served by this person. The prayer of quiet is symbolized by the water wheel, which delivers a much more water with a lot less work. Little effort is needed as a person puts their bucket under the water gushing out from the power of the water wheel. A person may realize they have received much in a short time in the prayer of quiet.

Spiritual directors in particular must be encouraged to recognize and affirm contemplation. Doctors of the church and our own experience tell us that it is frequently given, but an often ignored gift of God's love. In the fourth dwelling places of *The Interior Castle* Teresa makes a frequently quoted statement concerning one's practice of prayer: "The important thing is not to think much, but to love much and to do that which best stirs you to love."[33] A challenge to facilitators of contemplative prayer groups, who deal with introducing the prayer of simplicity to new members, is to simultaneously train former members to be sensitive to the action of the Holy Spirit within. This can be problematic when members do not realize that God beckons to a love beyond all methods. A person will not reach the prayer of union in the following dwelling places if they are attached to any particular method. Although Teresa deeply valued using a method of simplicity because it helped her immensely in her own prayer development, we are not surprised that John of the Cross taught no particular method. He did not want the focus to be on methods, but on sensitivity to God's action within.

---

33   Kavanaugh, Castle, 70.

5

Union in Love

While the Holy Spirit holds only the will in love in the prayer of quiet, *all the faculties* are held here, in the *prayer of union*. The story of Clare has in it the major elements of the prayer of union explained by Teresa in the fifth dwelling places. If the dwelling places seemed to overlap in chapters one through four, the smooth moving between chapters five through seven is even more obvious in this story. The reason the story of Clare was chosen here is because she experienced the fluctuations in prayer, which are typical in the fifth dwelling places.

Clare's Story

Clare had a difficult time with prayer for several years. In fact her experience was of the intense night of sense which opens out into the night of spirit. A brief comment in the talks of Father Keating and the position taken by Susan Muto brought this connection to my attention. This has been footnoted in chapter three.

After many of the interior trials she experienced, Clare was left with the inability to pray. Twice she experienced the wound of love Teresa calls a 'blow'. As if on pilgrimage, Clare visited the two places where this 'blow' took place. One was in a place used for a choir and the other was mid-way down a stairway Clare used to wash frequently. Clare remembered that each time this experience occurred, she cried out. She was happy no one was around because she knew she did not need medical attention. Shortly after this experience took place Clare thought it was like Jesus, being crushed under the cross during his third fall with mouth to the ground, breathing the dust beneath him. Later, she found it interesting that Teresa explains this experience with the words "being ground to dust as far as all worldly concerns."[34]

One day Clare found a volume of the *Cloud of Unknowing* left haphazardly on a chair in a library. She had been looking in every spiritual library for an answer to the prayer problem she experienced and with no results. This book at last held the answer for her. For the first time in many years Clare was able to understand how, when it comes to God, unknowing can be better than knowing. The book presented a method of prayer which Clare found rather easy. She sat for long hours simply letting God draw her into his love. At times Clare was deeply recollected even during work and felt she was like Martha and Mary, simultaneously doing her job while sitting at the feet of Jesus absorbed in his love. It was like Jesus took her on retreat.

During a time of interior temptations and trials, Clare had one moment which was more than just a consolation to get her through. It was a preview of a future prayer which would become her whole life of relationship with God and others. During adoration of the Blessed Sacrament, Jesus in the monstrance made known to Clare how He was in communion with the other persons of the Trinity within her. Now the prayer was not her own, but His.

After some time Clare met up with two significant people, a Franciscan sister, who recommended that she read *The Interior Castle* and a theologian. The theologian used the word 'circumincession' and Clare could explain what it was without ever having heard it previously. Nor had she spoken to a theologian before this time. She conveyed that 'circumincession' is the inner life of loving relationship within the Persons who are God. It is an interpenetration of those Persons, who beckon us to enter into and to share their life of loving relationship. The theologian was delighted because what Clare haltingly expressed at

---

34   Kavanaugh, *Castle*, 166-167.

the time, was a simple way of describing the dogma he taught in class. It was proof that true religious experience and dogma are not separate realities, but that they confirm and support one another.

The movement of Love, which is God's inner life within, is both entirely still and entirely dynamic. The nature of love is that it be poured out. Our prayer and ministry are modeled after this pattern of the Love in which we were created, a profound inner life of love that is shared. Because it is born out of an interpenetration of Persons, the Christian life is meant to be a consummation of spiritual love in community. All true love is an undeserved act of God's outpouring Love. Clare now saw the stability of relationship as taking place in God, gifted by God's mercy, and far beyond human personality, taken alone without God.

During this stage of her spiritual journey, there were fluctuations between consciousness of Love within and vaguely hearing what was going on around her. These alternated as long as Clare remained in prayer. She had heard that eventually even the sense of hearing might be alienated as one became more absorbed in God. It seemed to her that as in death, hearing is the last of the senses to go. A couple of times circumstances enabled Clare to find out that indeed, she had probably experienced this alienation.

Many years later Clare was on a long retreat. One morning after Holy Communion, she knew instantly that Jesus had taken her hand in an experience that seems more 'intellectual' than 'imaginative.' The divine gaze between Clare and Jesus seems to her to be indescribable. She says that only one who has had it will know all it brings with it. The difference between an *imaginative* and an *intellectual vision* will be explained in the following chapters. Like Esperanza, Clare permits this story to be told in the hope that it will help someone who reads it.

As the wise woman in the prayer group often reminded us, "Once you have been here in contemplation, there is no going back." Teresa and John of the Cross, in fact, explained this union with God, each from a different perspective. John said that once the will is in full union, as described in the sixth dwelling places, it is confirmed in grace. Teresa, on the other hand, expains that we always heve free will and that one is free to backslide at anytime.

Definition: The Prayer of Union

While the prayer of quiet unites the will of a person with the will of God in love for brief moments, the prayer of union unites the whole person with God. All the faculties, memory, intellect and will are now completely united with God. Since a person is not self-conscious during contemplation, we depend on the agreement of experts in the field of Mystical Theology to tell us that this prayer lasts for no more than half an hour. What one experiences is that there are no distractions when in the prayer of union. If there is time for a long prayer period, one experiences fluctuations from a time of no distractions to a time when one hears what is going on around them, but is oddly not at all disturbed by this. After a brief period, one will once again return to the prayer of union. This prayer is symbolized by Teresa as a tree planted near a living stream of water. The tree's very roots are inundated as are the person's faculties by the living presence of God within.

Teresa says the prayer of union is also like entering into a cocoon where one is willing to leave all to be transformed. Her story of the silkworm, building its own cocoon so as to be transformed in it by a kind of spiritual death, is the most well-known description of the prayer of union in the fifth dwelling places. Mystical death as described by Teresa is a most positive experience. She says that it is easier to die when one sees oneself living a new life.[35] *The Prayer of Full Union* will be described in the next chapter. In it the faculties will be held for a longer time and even the senses will participate in union. At times Teresa uses the terms *full union, ecstasy* and *rapture* in a way that is interchangeable.

Certitude

St. Bonaventure tells us that the certitude of faith is had in the experience of darkness. When it comes to religious experience, faith is the one important and stable constant. Teresa points out that the

---

35   Kavanaugh, Castle, 99.

certitude of one *being in God and God in them* is had in the prayer of union. Kavanaugh describes this certitude of the divine indwelling in the prayer of union, according to Teresa:

> *God so places Himself in the interior of that soul that when it returns to itself it can in no way doubt that it was in God and God was in it. This truth remains with it so firmly that even though years go by without God's granting that favor again, the soul can never forget nor doubt that it was in God and God was in it.*[36]

Teresa identifies this direct meeting with God of a human soul in its whole essence to the betrothal or espousal of that person with God. She explains both the *unknowing* element of the experience as well as the *inebriation* that is experienced. At first a person experiencing an encounter with God that involves all of their faculties expresses it as *I know not what.* Since there is no sensory participation in this experience, there are no words to describe it. From time to time one of the two faculties, memory or understanding, return to themselves. Then once again they are held in prayer until a time when both faculties are held so as to taste the divine wine of God's love that they are inebriated and bewildered by it. Several hours can seem like several minutes as God gathers up the faculties and draws them into his love time and again.

Spiritual Death

At first the moments of union are brief and the will can still be divorced from God in some of its decisions. Only God has the right to cut certain bonds as only God knows to what a person is inordinately attached. Here, in the prayer of union, one enters the cocoon and faces one's spiritual death perhaps several times in one prayer period. Later, in the sixth dwelling places, The Holy Spirit makes use of interior trials as well as secondary causes to detach the person.

Peers describes this state, the prayer of union, as *The Third Water* and a time of incipient union:

---

36   Ibid., 89.

It marks a new degree of infused contemplation, and a very high one.
By means of the most celebrated of all her metaphors, that of the silk-
worm, St. Teresa explains how far the soul can go to prepare itself for
what is essentially gift from God…for the first time, the faculties of
the soul are 'asleep'. It is of short duration, but while it lasts, the soul is
completely possessed by God.[37]

Estrangement

Following E. A. Peers description of the prayer of union, it is easy
to see why one experiencing it finds themselves estranged from the
things of this world:

In fact, for the time that this condition lasts the soul is without con-
sciousness as one usually knows it and has no power to think…in fact,
it has completely died to the world so that it may live more fully in
God…This is a delectable death, a snatching of the soul from all the
activities which it can perform while it is in the body; a death full of
delight.[38]

Spiritual directors, noticing that one has had this gift of espousal in
the prayer of union, especially the prayer of full union in the following
dwelling places, can safely assume that one is ready for a significant
ministry. So detached are they in God from *works* which others may
think of as their own. And so in full union with God the occasions
which might at first bring spiritual harm, do not do so.[39]

Martha and Mary Become One

Teresa sees the mercy of God as very much operative in the prayer
of union. A person here knows that the fruits of ministry are not one's
own. One begins to understand and guard heavenly treasures and to
want to share them. Teresa says that this person beseeches God not

---

37 Peers, Castle, introduction, xv-xvi.
38 Peers, Castle, 83
39 Kavanaugh, Castle, 104.

to be the only rich one. The gifts given here are seen by Teresa for the profit of many. She wishes that God would find someone better equipped than she herself is to share them.

An abundant inflowing of love comes from God's touch. One suffers from seeing God offended. One can become lost in God in all that was formerly of concern. Teresa sees the love of God as a heat that can be transmitted to others. It cannot be given away unless it is unselfish. Therefore, the analogy of the silkworm, dying to self to be transformed, is essential to Teresa's teaching: the goal of the contemplative life is good works.

Union with God for All

Having been created in the image of God and baptized in the Father, Son and Holy Spirit, it seems unthinkable that Christians would not consider union with God to be for all. We are told in Matthew that the Kingdom of Heaven is within. John and Paul also offer much mystical inspiration. Symbols such as the living water, which is represented on the cover of this book, need to be explored in Christian churches.

The Union of the Faculties

Far beyond just keeping the commandments, the gift of God in response to our desire for love, offers us much more than we could ask or imagine. Our response to God's gift of Love opens us up to a greater consciousness of what it means to be Christian in a world devoid of true love. The experience of love in the prayer of union puts order into all of the loves of our lives. The faculties which are purified in *the night of the spirit* are first held in union here in the fifth dwelling places. Then they are purged *in the obscure dark night of spirit* so that they might serve while held in habitual union.

The *quality* of service is determined by *what one loves*. It is the inner life poured out, that results in a transformative change in our culture. Personality alone without love does little. One does not just become aware that there is life beyond personality. Evangelization needs to include an awareness of the spiritual level of Scripture along with instruction on the *sacramental mysticism of Baptism*. *The Interior Castle* focuses on the indwelling presence of God in the souls of all people and the gradual active presence of God in the souls of the just. When all the faculties of a person are moved by God, only then can significant work in the world be accomplished.

Signposts - Fifth Dwelling Places

In the fifth dwelling places prayer may be longer with fluctuations between the prayer of union and the prayer of quiet.. There is a certitude of faith even and especially in darkness. The certitude that one is in God and God is in the soul is the outstanding sign of the prayer of union. One may have an experience of inebriation, a profound interior joy, as well as of estrangement from participation in the things of this world.

Since all the faculties are held by the Holy Spirit the fifth dwelling places, there are no distractions as compared to the kind of union had in the prayer of quiet in which one may be plagued by many thoughts . However, since the prayer of union lasts for no more than half an hour, the person slips back into the prayer of quiet and alternates between the two should there be a longer time for silent prayer. Teresa holds this prayer in such esteem that she says one should be extremely grateful if having experienced it only once in their lifetime.

Spiritual Practices - Fifth Dwelling Places

The only role of the person in the fifth dwelling places is to be receptive. Self-knowledge is always important as it is the food to be eaten with every bread, however dainty. Works of charity and union with God's will are conditions required to truly be in the prayer of union. As the prayer of union becomes intense it easily moves into the prayer of simple ecstasy discussed in the following chapter.

Conclusion

In the fifth dwelling places all the faculties are held in union for brief periods. Martha and Mary become one. That is, the active and contemplative life are consciously joined as a person goes about their day aware that they operate not only on the level of daily work, but also on a deeper level of conscious union with God. Teresa's analogy of the silkworm has much to teach us about all transitions in life. If Teresa, using her image of the silkworm, realizes that new life comes from a transition involving death, she sees that the silkworm is willing to enter into its cocoon in order to die to its old form and come out entirely changed. The analogy provides a motivation during painful transitions in our own lives, when if we cooperate with the new life that seems to be God's will, we can more easily come out a new creation.

As the intensity of the prayer of union increases, even the senses are held in union in the prayer of ecstasy. This new developmental stage of contemplative prayer has many dwelling places. In it, Teresa covers the types of religious experience any number of people may or may not have. These may be mere awakenings at any stage of the spiritual journey and may not at all be connected to the sixth dwelling places. Or the experiences here may be an integral part of the sixth dwelling places. Here Teresa will introduces for the first time, the difference between *imaginative* and *intellectual* experiences.

6

Selfless Love

In addition to ecstasy, in which God beckons the faculties and senses to participate in the full union of love, Teresa describes a great many phenomenal experiences in the sixth dwelling places. At the time of Teresa and John of the Cross phenomenal experience was a monumental problem. For this reason Teresa spends significant time on this topic and its discernment. Here she also begins to speak of the superior nature of *intellectual* religious experience. In these eleven chapters, comprising some sixty pages, it is easy for beginners to get the idea that *The Interior Castle* is mainly about phenomenal experience.

Angie's Story

Angie was a party girl. Her celebrations always had a theme as they hung together in a carefully coordinated tapestry of food, games and good cheer. However, Angie was having a serious spiritual challenge. She brought it to several people, experts in church work, who said it would go away. It did not. Angie sat one day in the Bible class which she really liked to attend and gently pounded her clenched fist on the side of her head. She met with the teacher for a private session and stated her problem.

For the longest time Angie could not remember a thing taught in the class, in a homily, or related to anything spiritual. Her new spiritual director, who was also the Scripture teacher, knew that the flip side of the *Cloud of Unknowing* is *the cloud of forgetting*. In these sixth dwelling places, the night of the spirit is the most significant element. It includes both the unknowing and forgetting of spiritual concepts once greatly cherished. Although people reading the sixth dwelling places with little experience usually think that the phenomenal experiences related there are the most significant thing, what is really essential is the complete purification of the faculties, memory, intellect and will. A person who studies frequently may notice that they can read phonetically, but cannot understand the written words on a page of Scripture. A person, like Angie, who learns mainly from listening to homilies and classes at church will notice the inability to retain what was heard. Both are signs of the dark night of the spirit.

For Angie, most painfully, the *cloud of forgetting* was problematic. Angie was briefly introduced to the method of *The Cloud of Unknowing*, which is in effect, the prayer of simplicity. Anyone who is attracted to it may use this form of prayer. In the dark night of the spirit it is the only thing that works. The entire Bible Class spent five minutes in silent prayer each time they met for class. Angie often told the story about how she watched a bug on the floor at first as she was not used to silent prayer. Soon, without prodding, her prayer practice became one hour per day in silent prayer. Angie was given a small book called *Common Mystic Prayer* by Dieffenbach, ofm. cap. She noticed that it objectified what she talked about in spiritual direction. With this help, Angie launched a contemplative life that was extremely fruitful for herself and others.

Before long there was a serious illness in Angie's family. She realized that a male relative would never come home again if she did not care for him. She brought the problem to the contemplative prayer group as she had misgivings about caring for a man to whom she was not married. The group encouraged her to do this ministry as it is what nurses do all of the time.

Angie loved to say the rosary and was invited by another group to join them, which she did. She noticed the group promoting phenomenal experience in a way that was not healthy and so she would not join in. Jesus showed Angie he was pleased, as often happens with people who stand alone for what is right. Angie reported this to her spiritual director, but did not consider this gentle look of Jesus her most powerful religious experience.

One time when Angie was taking care of her sick relative she saw Jesus in his eyes. This experience went with Angie to her death. She knew that she would soon be looking back at Jesus just like that, only it would be even better and forever. An incurable form of cancer would challenge Angie's faith life, as well as that of all who loved her. At one time the medications given to her caused depression, but when she was no longer on it, Angie returned to her fun-loving self.

Angie taught the contemplative prayer group a mini course on *The Spiritual Canticle* of John of the Cross. Her favorite lines were about how the Beloved, looking at the soul, impresses His image on her. And the two rejoice in this image together: *When you looked at me your eyes imprinted your grace in me; for this you loved me ardently and thus my eyes deserved to adore what they beheld in you...*John of the Cross goes on to explain that the eyes here are the purified faculties of the soul. This adoration and every work becomes meritorious in the grace of God.[40]

This look of love, this divine gaze, was already in this life, part of Angie's spiritual experience. Mirroring this transforming moment, as spiritual directors are inclined to do, the two shared it powerfully. Angie no longer feared death. The young priest who celebrated Angie's funeral Mass said he knew Angie did not fear death, but he did not know why. The honor of sharing her knowledge of *the loving look of Jesus*, especially at the time of death, is one of the most rewarding any spiritual director could have. John of the Cross and Teresa of Avila taught that those who met God this intimately during the course of life, experience death as *a gentle rapture*. It is a continuation of their experience of God, that loving divine gaze known even during this life.

From time to time Angie expressed a sorrow that she could not

---

40   Kavanaugh, *Spiritual Canticle of St. John of the Cross in Complete Works*, stanza 32, 599-601.

be with us longer. She would have much to add to our ministry. We assured her that we believed in the communion of saints. Our wise woman in the group, who always had powerful one-liners said, *Angie has much to teach us about death.* Her family asked that we use Angie's real name in this story. It is the only one like it. Indeed, the message of the final dwelling places is that those who are transformed do not fear death. It is the loving look of Jesus that transforms us. Angie's life and death encourage us to be habitually ready to return the loving look of Jesus, whose love continually beckons. Father Lawrence Freeman once said that Jesus always looks at us with love. "Intimacy happens when we look back." Everyone has the potential of being transformed by the loving look of Jesus. It seems no one has ever told us this before now. How depressing it was to think that we would have to wait for death to experience union with God. An understanding of baptism, communion, Scripture and the spiritual masters God has provided have changed life on this earth to an exciting adventure into the mystery of God.

Purification of the Faculties

Charmed by the divine operation in the fifth dwelling places, the faculties are prepared for their further purification in the dark night of the spirit. The faculties must be made simple in all things spiritual, so that they can be united to God who is essentially simple. This is most significant in the sixth dwelling places. It is a point often missed. The outpouring of the unconscious and the voiding of the faculties, intellect, memory and will are the essence of the sixth dwelling places.

> *Through contemplation, God: empties the human faculties of their natural objects in order to fill them with His light and love; purifies the deeply rooted imperfections in the human spirit that it might be united with the Spirit of God; frees a person from attachment to self and to one's own activity and transforms the human faculties, affections, and appetites into a divine mode of acting; communicates directly,*

intimately, and secretly with a person in the highest degree of prayer; and conducts the soul along the road to union with God in love.[41]

Here Kevin Culligan quotes from *The Obscure Dark Night,* book two of *The Dark Night of John of the Cross,* pointing out that contemplation itself is the soul's guide to God. *This union is implicitly the goal of spiritual direction as a helping process.*[42]

Outpouring of the Unconscious

*It bears repeating that d*uring the course of life we collect a lot of *crud.* It is collected in the form of interior baggage. Unknowingly good people repress even more than they acknowledge. Holding onto toxic psychic material, which is not appropriately released, blocks union with God. The outpouring of the unconscious often occurs during times of silence. Some in contemplative prayer groups say that right after Holy Communion the weirdest thoughts occur to them from an unknown place within. It is obviously not from their will, as they find this disturbing. Now they must hold on *at a deeper level* while gently letting go of thoughts that are not desired. This deeper level of consciousness is the level of contemplation. Contraries cannot coexist. The divine action within heals the soul by pushing out its hidden stains. Having successfully endured this ordeal, one will find it possible to remain at this deeper level of consciousness even during exterior conflicts.

Hoffman addresses the outpouring of the unconscious as one of the most painful purifications of the interior life. He explains with understanding and compassion the purpose of this interior trial: "And so many things come out. The all but total rebellion of the creature against the limitations of being a creature, against the limitations at least of being the kind of creature which must conform to a law other than its own, which must give up the complete freedom he desires so intensely is now seen."[43] The definition, psychological aspects and

---

41 Culligan, diss., 339.
42 Ibid., 338.
43 Dominic Hoffman, *The Life Within: The Prayer of Union* (New York: Sheed and Ward, 1965), 119
    See also chapter 10 on "Psychological Aspects of Passive Purification", 109-153.

spiritual benefits of the outpouring of the unconscious will follow. This process must be understood in order to prevent further blockage of the stored up material, which prevents spiritual growth.

Definition: Outpouring of the Unconscious

The outpouring of the unconscious is a purifying experience. It removes the roots of strong emotion, prideful desire for perfection, natural, but not willful rebellion against God's will for us and anything unconsciously or consciously repressed from our past. It is accompanied by deep humility at the sight of so much evil emerging from within oneself. It requires a manly strength and courage, even when experienced by a woman. For this reason not all are gifted with this experience. The outpouring of the unconscious begins when the Holy Spirit knows one is ready to endure it. The reorganization of one's entire interior life commences and one has the feeling that if they can survive it, they will be in an entirely different place. It is ultimately a place of peace and inner joy. Only the Holy Spirit can combine suffering with joy and peace. The silence of contemplation is not the workplace of the evil one. Uninformed people will avoid silence because they believe this falsehood. John of the Cross assures us that one is safe in the dark night. The self before this conversion has set up its own glorification as the partially hidden goal of all it does. The false perfectionism of always being right, along with past resentments must be rooted out. This is the work of the Holy Spirit in the sixth dwelling places.

Psychological Aspects: Outpouring of the Unconscious

Now that the hidden content of one's inner life is out there, the experience is one of a great *void* and *longing for God*. This differs from psychological depression in which there is no longing for God, but just displeasure with everything. Here in this passive purification, one is psychologically and physically tired. One feels psychologically 'rattled'. Walking in a fog of *unknowing,* one can usually function quite normally. Acts of charity can always be performed. This is in contrast to a case of depression where selfishness predominates. Now all healing must come directly from God. This is accomplished by the direct action of the Holy Spirit within know as *contemplation*. Self-help programs will not work if the dark night is in progress. The *humility* of one seeking therapy is probably the most valuable tool for healing. It never hurts to seek help. When *working on oneself* leaves one flat and produces no spiritual movement, this may be the time to seek experienced spiritual guidance. Without further knowledge about the dark night of the soul, a person may believe that it is the humble thing to keep actively *striving* even with no results. Just as one is always free to change a medical doctor when treatment is not productive, one may also be called upon to change a spiritual course, which is meant for beginners, but now does not work.

When in spiritual darkness a person is not initially conscious of the transition taking place. It may be time to seek out a director who is aware of it. The transition will ultimately involve a simpler form of prayer, faithfulness in dryness and a willingness to accept even moments of *contemplative sweetness*, which is very different from discursive satisfaction. Here one knows one cannot do anything by oneself and admitting that, accepts joyfully from the hand of God whatever is given. A great peace fills the space within, which formerly may have been occupied by powerfully intense outpouring of the unconscious. The most intense forms of these trials are rarely experienced. One must find a director to whom they can tell all. However, this need not be done in great detail.

Having studied the dark nights with insights from John of the Cross, Muto, Hoffman and Keating, it is possible to conclude that the *intense night of sense* leads to the *night of spirit* through *the outpouring of the unconscious*. Further, some are called to experience and eventually let go of, the pain caused by sin and held in *the collective unconscious*. This was the experience of Mother Theresa of Calcutta. It is also the experience of people today. One can see why Teresa insists that we focus on the humanity of Jesus in order to make it through to the final dwelling places. In his humanity Jesus experienced the grief caused by sin and held in the collective consciousness of all mankind.

When one cannot pray, works of charity may distract one a bit from the psychological pressure of an intense passive dark night. This includes an experience of outpouring from the personal or collective unconscious. When possible the person does well to run into the arms of God in all of his nakedness. Some have found relief kneeling before a crucifix or an image of Mary. Evil cannot touch those protected by Jesus and his mother. Complete healing will be done by the Holy Spirit alone. It is done in the individual and in the culture as well. The peace experienced at this time of surrender may well be symbolized by black velvet. It is dark, but soft. The prayer of faith reaches its climax in the *night of spirit*. This is discussed in the sixth dwelling places of *The Interior Castle*.

Symbolism may be used where mere words fall short in expressing religious experience. For example, one may consider the pillar of fire by night and the cloud by day in the book of Exodus. These represented the special presence of God that guided the Israelites. The intense form of the *cloud of unknowing* does not last forever. Trees totally stripped of their leaves will regain their beauty as the seasons change. Yet, a person must be willing to stay in this darkness and total stripping of self as long as God wills, even if it seems like it might last forever. This is referred to as the *passive dark night of spirit*. A scene taken from a natural disaster where everything as far as the eye can see is left barren is an apt image, depicting how a person feels in this *obscure dark night*. The will, memory and intellect, having been purified and simplified from human complexity, can now become one with God. The Christian seeks union with God who is formless and entirely simple. In this total purification of the faculties John of the Cross rejoices, calling this *a most happy, glad night* in which the soul is made one with God. The *castle* and the *night* are only two of the many symbols used in the history of Christian mysticism. *Love Beckons* limits its scope to these two, employing others such as *the cloud of unknowing* where they are helpful. Using such symbolism promotes comfort in the realization that *spiritual darkness* can be *a positive experience*. This will lead on some level, for everyone who embraces it, to the fullness of light.

Spiritual Benefits: Outpouring of the Unconscious

It is commonly held that many enter the prayer of quiet, but few go beyond it. An accurate understanding of the passive states which follow the prayer of quiet facilitates this passage. Through *the passive dark night of spirit* there is a liberation from the unconscious emotional drives, fears and resentments one has carried as heavy baggage for too long. Pride in the intellect is reduced, while one is no longer subject to a false idealization of oneself. Now God is allowed to make the advances in prayer. A person is united in will, in simple silence and attentiveness to God's action within. Since one could not get oneself out of the painful darkness, one is more likely to trust God, maybe even one's spiritual director, for the rest of the spiritual journey.

In the night of sense the rational intellect, fed by the senses, does not work on spiritual material. The intuitive intellect still works, but can also be a cause for hidden pride. Since God is simple, even the intuitive intellect and the faculties of memory, and will must be further purified along with the deepest roots of the sense life. John of the Cross and Teresa refer to this action of purification as *an impediment* to the natural functioning of the faculties as applied to the spiritual life. They use the word 'impedir' to describe the divine action of God which takes hold of the faculties, purifies them and makes them ready to receive God in all simplicity. Now one is guided by the loving awareness of God alone and not primarily from any outside source.

Impediment to Memory, Intellect and Will

John of the Cross uses most of his 'impedir' statements in Book Two of *The Dark Night*. This section on *The Dark Night of the Spirit* can be found translated in E.A. Peers who says it is the imperfections in the soul which *impede* it from enjoying delectable contemplation.

In N2, 6:3 John reminds us that one entering the dark night is forsaken by creatures, particularly friends. There are no secondary supports. Nor can one in the experience attempt a clear description. John of the Cross, however, is quite the friend who does understand. He gets right to the point in many of his passages on the dark nights. In this passage he says that emptiness and poverty are experienced on every level. In the miseries of one's own imperfection, aridity, void and thick darkness, one is suspended as if hanging in mid-air, with no support and little ability to breathe.

In N2, 8:1 we are told that this night of spirit *impedes the natural work of the faculties and affections.* The result is a profound *emptiness*, a *loneliness* that nothing but God can fill. During this time one cannot beseech God or raise the mind and affections. It is as if a cloud passes in front of the soul. John of the Cross uses the word 'cloud' sixteen times in his writing. It is very likely he was aware of the fourteenth century work *The Cloud of Unknowing,* which is extremely valuable to one who wishes to understand this stage of the spiritual journey. Although *The Living Flame* and *The Spiritual Canticle* of St. John of the Cross can be quite ecstatic, yet John of the Cross sees everything short of the spiritual marriage and the beatific vision as part of the dark night.

In N 2, 14:1-2 we are told that in this divine operation of uncreated grace God puts to sleep all the members of one's household, faculties, passions, affections and appetites. The natural operations of the human being, the activities of intellect and sense are compared to the enemies of one's own household.[44] One's own pride and the evil spirit can operate through these faculties, but they have no power in this dark night of faith. In N2, 15:11 John of the Cross compares the *escape* both from his external prison in the dark of night and from his more real interior enemies as described above. In this night the soul subtly escapes from its enemies by the secret ladder, living faith, by which it departs securely and successfully.

Continuing on in N 2, 16:2 we see that individuals *are freed from error* because in the night of the spirit their human operations and affections are impeded. They, as well as the world and the devil, have no other means of warring against them except through the faculties and senses. In regard to this operation of uncreated love, John mentions in the same book N2, 16:3 that only the goods of union with God are imparted to the appetites because they are not now distracted with

---

44   Lam 3:44.

useless and harmful things: vainglory, presumption, pride, false joy and may other evils.

Finally, N2:23 the value of *the secret nature* of this divine operation is supremely valued above every other gift, even though it be supernatural, but imparted through the senses. The superior part of the soul is united to God in secret. The soul will eventually come to esteem the direct touch of God's divinity above all God's other favors. In darkness the soul is secure because evil enters only through the senses and easily compromised human faculties.

For this reason, phenomenal experience which relies on the senses, and which according to John of the Cross *may be* supernatural, should not be desired. Groups which promote phenomenal experience will stay clear of the teaching of John of the Cross, which they falsely see as preventing the growth of their members. This is very dangerous as unlearned, uninformed, but spiritually inclined good natured people are often swept up into such groups. The dark faith of John of the Cross does not appeal to them and so they are taking others with them on a course which is bound for shipwreck. They are inclined to think that, since a spiritual director perhaps does not have their experience, they are above guidance. It is clearly a case of pride. When a phenomenal experience they have set up in their own minds does not occur or has been proven false, they are deflated like a huge helium balloon. It is likely that there is no *stable source* of indwelling uncreated grace at the center of their experience.

Teresa of Avila, who learned how to balance her religious experience through the influence of John of the Cross, also uses the term *impedir* in chapter eleven, which is the final chapter of the sixth dwelling places. In her desire for God over the years, Teresa realizes that everything but God is mere dust. She comes to experience this suddenly by a wound much deeper than anything physical, which she calls a 'blow' and which makes one cry out although the pain is not physical. With this experience she tells us that God can detach one in an instant from things which we ourselves could never detach. [45] Clare, in chapter

---

45   Kavanaugh, Castle, 166-167.

five having this experience and not having read Teresa's description of it, never forgot it and valued it so much that she went back to visit the places in which this painfully precious experience took place. In the sixth dwelling places everything but God becomes dust and ashes. Experiencing this becomes more valuable than the spiritual delights of initial contemplation. Although it is valuable to learn the full significance of such an experience, the person somehow intuits their value in a general way, possibly even before having it confirmed from a spiritual master such as Teresa of Avila or John of the Cross.

One can see that in Teresa the description here is far more personal and concrete than that which John of the Cross gives. However, the examples of *impedir* are clear in both. It is a matter of style. Both the style and teaching of Teresa and John are extremely helpful. The binding of the faculties causes a 'void' that creates a strange solitude that no creature can fill. Teresa tells us that she believes no earthy or heavenly creature is meant to fill this emptiness, which is meant to be filled by the One alone who is Love. Ultimately, God is the One in whom all of our loves reside, though one may not as yet realize it.

Teresa uses the story in John 4 of the woman at the well, saying the soul is on fire with a thirst which is unendurable, but which can only be taken away with the water of which the Lord speaks. Thus in the account of Teresa we see graphically depicted the intense personal longing of the soul for union with God. Nothing else can substitute for it although people sometimes spend all their life with searches that terminate in unfulfilled dead ends.

In the sixth dwelling places Teresa tells us that God Himself, the true Comforter, consoles one, taking away the intense longing for love. She tells us that the form of the intellect must be made unto God, Who is without form. She describes the kinds of consolations God gives in great detail so that directors of souls may know how to discern what is truly of God in these matters. A person is never a good judge in their own case. Indeed, Teresa and John tell us that when the form of the intellect is changed, a person is not self-conscious, which means it cannot judge itself, or even at times follow the judgment of the spiritual director. One will probably see mainly one's faults, but will listen to the director. Thus it is easy to discern the false from the true mystic. *Self-knowledge, the bread eaten with every food however dainty,* leads to *humility* and a spirit of obedience to the solid teaching of the Church as found in the Christian mystics.

The Dark Night of the Spirit and Ecstasy

Eventually even John of the Cross admits the existence of *ecstasy* while elaborating on it extensively in *The Living Flame of Love* and *The Spiritual Canticle*. In his commentary on *The Living Flame* John of the Cross says that one can imagine from what the faculties suffer when they are voided, how much they must rejoice and take delight when they are filled with God. Evelyn Underhill, who had a penchant for writing on the stage of ecstasy, was awarded a fellowship from Oxford University in the early 1900's. There she produced her monumental work in which she agrees with Teresa that ecstasy goes beyond the true self, beyond the cloud of unknowing and into the mystery of God. Here divine love draws one out of self and into unnamed Being. She identifies this meeting with God as a culminating point of contemplation in which a final and unforgettable knowledge of God is characteristically imparted by means of an *intellectual vision*, a term which will be considered in Chapter Seven. Underhill notes the good effects of ecstasy and rapture as: vitality, lucidity and supreme intuition regarding God and the things of God.[46] Those who want to equate self-hypnosis with contemplation cannot come up with a list of effects regarding self-hypnosis which is this significant.

Ecstasy does have some physical side-effects which may be helpful to consider. As one grows in contemplation the breath may slow down, even to the point of preventing one from talking. Heaviness in the limbs impede movement. As has been mentioned, with the alienation of the senses, the hearing is the last to be lost. However, these accidental aspects of ecstasy will disappear in the seventh dwelling places.

---

46   Kavanaugh, *Living Flame of Love in Collected Works John of the Cross*, 680.
      Cf Underhill, ibid., 363-370.

When one is concerned about not being as active as one formerly was, the spiritual director needs to say, "This *will* get integrated." This is not the time to change one's life style. The ministry of a person who has experienced passive contemplation will benefit greatly in the long run. No amount of professional preparation can compare with the positive effect of God's action within when it comes to effective ministry.

Phenomenal Experience

Taken by itself phenomenal experience is probably the least transformative element considered in the sixth dwelling places. Yet, it is important to know that directees will only bring it to a director they trust. On a larger scale, at times, it may be necessary for the Church as a whole to accept cerain approved phenomena in order to get the attention of believers and refocus them on the essentials found in Scripture. As a spiritual director, one finds that phenomenal experience, sometimes called extraordinary experience, is given momentarily to encourage us in practicing the faith or in doing good works, especially in difficult circumstances.

Hyacinth's Story Continued

Hyacinth was such a person. Her mother explained to her that fragrances experienced after a spiritual work of mercy were a sign that God and Our Lady were pleased. The first time a fragrance captivated Hyacinth she was walking with her mother from a devotional service at church in the direction of a huge nursery where flowers were sold. It was perhaps a mile away. The first thing Hyacinth thought was to wonder what powerfully fragrant flowers they had at Frank's Nursery and Crafts. Her mother explained that one could not smell flowers at such a distance, but that Mary was pleased with the rosary they had just said together with other members of the parish.

The next time this occurred Hyacinth was walking through the foyer of the church with the facilitator of the prayer group. She was secretly wondering how to tell her she was going to give up silent prayer. Suddenly the beautiful fragrance of flowers overwhelmed her.

She began to check out the flowers in the entrance of the church. They were all silk. Hyacinth knew God was pleased with her continuing her quiet prayer and she did not give it up.

At other times Hyacinth noticed that she was strengthened in the doing of good works with a fragrance she could only think of as spiced and fragrant wine. It was like the sweet inebriation provided by the Beloved in *The Spiritual Canticle of John of the Cross*. Still, at other times, Hyacinth was affirmed in the doing of good works when others mentioned that they experienced a fragrance in close proximity to these spiritual or corporal works of mercy. Hyacinth thought that she would not know what they were talking about had she not experienced this first. Hyacinth wanted the readers to know that just because some of her experiences with fragrances are very interesting, they were not her deepest God experiences. Thus, she allowed several stories to be told.

Hyacinth was always devoted to working for people. Her social work took her to a poor neighborhood where the clients often had to wait outdoors before the building opened. However, in inclement weather all of the people were allowed into the ground floor of the building. When there was rain on hot and muggy days the perspiring people seemed packed together like cattle. It was difficult for staff to make their way through to the stairwell where their offices were. That whole year was a painful one for Hyacinth. The clients she was assigned to were troubled and some of the staff were conflicted, too. She wondered how she would ever make it through until her retirement. The fragrant sweet spice of the Bridegroom followed her everywhere that pertained to work. This day it was pouring rain with great intensity. Hyacinth dreaded pushing her way through the steamy hot corridor with its sweaty drenched bodies. As soon as she opened the door an unusually pleasant fragrance accompanied her through the entire, long hallway. She asked the cleaning lady what she had used. "Nothing that good," *w*as the reply.

Hyacinth made her way up to what was now a general office, but which used to be her own space the year before. It could have been full of negative remembrances, but it, too, was filled with a heavenly spiced fragrance. She mentioned the wonderful smell to the other social workers. "Yes," they said, "The coffee does smell good." On and on, pumping gas on the way to the social center or entering a room where someone had given her a hard time, Hyacinth experienced the fragrant presence of her Beloved. She finally realized that God used this means to get her through tough times.

Hyacinth wished to share another type of story because it gives an example of the Holy Spirit, affirming a good work by means of fragrance noticed by others. Hyacinth said that she had several of this type, but that she would again share the one that seemed most interesting. There were a couple of poor people who lived next door. They really needed help with maintaining their living quarters. At the time, Hyacinth was able to afford a few thousand dollars to help them. One Saturday morning Hyacinth was wondering about the prudence of giving away such a large sum of money all at once. As she slammed the door of her car shut she thought to herself, "Yet, I think Jesus is pleased with this idea." As she sat at the counter of her favorite coffee house, one of the waitresses asked her what she was wearing. "Nothing," replied Hyacinth. "I just had my hair cut. I don't think they put anything special on it." "Well," said the waitress, "You see the waitress in the far corner of the room? She smells it, too." By this time Hyacinth knew it was God's way of affirming her in this project. Without letting on, she thanked Jesus in her heart for affirming a good work which was usually beyond her means. The plan for the remodeling project to help her neighbors went very smoothly. Although it was nearing retirement, Hyacinth did not miss the money at this time or even after she retired.

Jane's Story

Jane was another person who experienced a phenomenal experience. Hers was a story of the *cyclical type* of dark night experienced by many. Jane benefitted profoundly from the study of John of the Cross and soon she could not even remember the darkness that once filled her with the fear of continual return. Once during her private prayer at home Jane felt herself *lifted up* off her chair. The experience of levitation is not as common as that of other phenomenal experiences. It is said that in such an experience the soul is so moved to God that the body must follow. At other times it is possible for one to feel lifted up in public and then Jane wanted to know if it is permitted to hold oneself down so as not to become a spectacle for others to see. A good answer would be that Teresa of Avila tried to hold herself down, but for her it did not work. So if it works, that is fine. At times we hear stories of those who feel lifted up and they are looking down at their own bodies. They return with an entirely new way of looking at things which they would like to share with others.

Upon completing my dissertation on the divine operation in *The Interior Castle,* I was told the story of a priest who wondered why his altar was getting shorter. He did not at first realize he was having a levitation. This kind of experience comes upon one when least expected. They are never authentic when people try to produce them. They are taken lightly by spiritual directors and are neither to be encouraged, nor to be put down by a director, who most probably has never experienced them personally. The reason for this is that the *focus* is to be *on union with God* and not on experiences. Teresa encourages us to hold gently the experiences of others that are authentic, even if they not ours or anything like our own. A person whose experience is real will not *flaunt it.* For this *humility* on the part of one who has the experience as well as the one who does not, gives God the credit for doing many things we do not fully understand.

Another fairly common experience spoken of extensively in the sixth dwelling places of *The Interior Castle* is that of the *imaginative vision* and the *locution.* Teresa gives examples of how these can be helpful and yet they can be deceptive. They do not remain part of one's spiritual life forever, but are, as we have said, helps to get one through trying times. Then they are quickly forgotten, as they should be, because they have already done their work. Supernatural imaginative visions take place because God stoops to our level of knowing through the senses. These are subject to error. These visions are called *extraordinary* because this is not God's ordinary way of acting. It is difficult to interpret the meaning of an imaginative vision. When they indicate some future event one must wait to see how the circumstances will play themselves out. Another challenge is in dealing with those who try to promote phenomenal experience, seeing it as an end in itself. In severe cases of obsession with imaginative visions medical therapy may be recommended.

The intellectual vision, which is different and rare, imparts something of God's essence. It is beyond error, is never forgotten and becomes part of one's entire way of life. Teresa introduces this concept in the sixth dwelling places and takes it up once again in the seventh. T It is referred to by John of the Cross, not as a *vision* at all, but as *substantial knowledge.* Here in the sixth dwelling places Teresa speaks of Our Lord walking beside her for many days. She did not see his features. However, she *knew* who he was. This *certitude* was of *his abiding presence* although she could not say *how* she knew it was Jesus. This is the first time Teresa speaks of an *intellectual* vision.

Keep Your Eyes Fixed on Jesus

Teresa noticed in her own life an error which we run into today. People who practice contemplative forms of prayer are led to believe that they should no longer think about Jesus. Teresa admits that this belief caused her much unnecessary dryness. One does not need to think of Jesus discursively in order to keep one's eyes fixed on Him. It is quite a simple gaze between Jesus and a soul, a gaze of love, which does one much good. "Life is long, and there are in it many trials... We need to look at Christ our model, how He suffered them, and also at His apostles and saints, so as to bear these trials with perfection."[47] If we could take but one message from the entire sixth dwelling places, the longest section of *The Interior Castle,* this would be it. Teresa firmly believed that those who do not fix their eyes on Jesus never make it to the final dwelling places. In order to do so one must learn to love the cross and must rely on Jesus as a model of perfection.

---

47   Kavanaugh, Castle, 149.

Signposts - Sixth Dwelling Places

Deep humility always accompanies valid religious experience. Interior trials and baffling illnesses may produce patience in the sixth dwelling places. The truest sign that a vision or locution is from God is that it effects what it says. At times the intellect and memory do not work on spiritual concepts in the sixth dwelling places. Wounds of love are treasured more than the spiritual delights in the prayer of quiet. The evil spirit does not produce deep interior joy simultaneously with suffering. Only the Holy Spirit can do this. Phenomenal experiences most often help people carry on at the moment in difficulties and then are quickly forgotten, as they should be, because they have already accomplished their work.

Spiritual Practices - Sixth Dwelling Places

Teresa advocates that we learn to be *indifferent to blame or praise* for there are as many people against as in favor of a person. When interior trials are great, one may not be able to pray, but one can always practice works of charity. When a spiritual insight involves some action to be taken, consult with a learned and prudent servant of God. Be disposed as soft wax, allowing Christ's image to be impressed in you, however He wishes. Cooperate with God's gifts with courage. People will either praise Him or criticize you. In either case you will benefit. Keep your eyes fixed on Jesus, who will take you *home* to His community of love with the Father and the Holy Spirit. When held in prayer often, consider making a list of practical obligations in advance. Then when you are able to move about, check them off as efficiently as you can.

Conclusion

The sixth dwelling places consist of eleven chapters of great interest to spiritual directors of contemplatives. Growing in the contemplative life for many years, individuals may also find in it answers to perplexing problems encountered on their own spiritual journey. These chapters deal with an understanding of detachment from spiritual things. This may be hard for people to understand. Spiritual things and spiritual experiences are *not* God. Therefore, we gratefully accept from God whatever is given, but especially and ultimately it is *the gift of God*, not secondary gifts, that we treasure. The sixth dwelling places deal with a sense of ultimate void and spiritual death as well as with a great variety of extraordinary phenomena, how to understand them and how to be detached from them. The purification of the faculties in the *dark night of the spirit* is explained as *unformation* in the teaching of Kees Waaijman. His expertise in the writings of John of the Cross rightly identifies this as crucial in discerning *the night of spirit*. It is necessary so that union with God's mode of being, which is formless, can take place.

Teresa begins to explain the kernel of religious experience in her presentation on *intellectual vision,* which she carries over into the seventh dwelling places. In it one enters into the mystery of God. For all the details persons may give concerning imaginative visions, one never discerns that they have learned anything experientially about the *essence of God* .Unlike humans, God's essence and God's attributes are one and the same. Both Teresa of Avila and John of the Cross value *intellectual vision,* called *substantial knowledge* in John of the Cross, as the kernel of truth to be discerned in religious experience. In these dwelling places Teresa shows her preference for intellectual vision as a means of entry into the mystery of God. This type of religious experience is not subject to error. In the spiritual classic *The Philokalia* we are told that the term 'theologian' is not applied to any individual unless they have this experience of the mystery of God. In this way their teaching is balanced with a sense of the Truth that no smooth arguments can erase from their consciousness. In order to experience God, the faculties must first become simple because God is simple. This is what the divine action accomplishes in *the dark night of the spirit.* As the main topic of consideration in the sixth dwelling places, darkness prepares us, as far as possible in this life, to enter the mystery of God.

7

Transformation in Love

We Long to See Your Face

The intense human desire to see the face of God, or to know God from experience, is found everywhere in Scripture. This is a reason to promote the mystical sense of Scripture, as we long to return to that sense of God in which we were created.

Father John's Story

As a parish priest, Father John made a yearly retreat. On one of these occasions he experienced the love of Jesus on the cross. This vision was 'intellectual' in that it was an experience of *the essence of God* as unconditional love. He was not concerned about describing how Jesus *looked*, but rather in sharing *the love that Jesus imparts*. Unconditional love is the *essence of God*. It is without form because *God is simple and formless*. This was something that remained with Father John as significant. It is the basis for his never wanting to hurt anyone. Others accept correction easily when they perceive the motivation is unconditional love. We have all heard that *God is Love* many times. We see it on bookmarks, stationery and even on tote bags. We hear sermons on the fourth gospel and the epistles of John. But to see it *from God's perspective* in an intellectual vision and to hear about it merely using our human faculties is an entirely different experience.

We always hear that a good teacher can come down to our level. Yet, there are excellent teachers who can tell when the student is ready to be raised up to their level. This is what God does in an intellectual vision. In it a person is, through purified faculties, raised to the knowledge of God in God. This *seeing* is the knowledge of *connaturality* by which all things in the seventh dwelling places are known by a kind of mutuality with God, which is not deserved, but freely given as gift.

Father John may not have realized that his demeanor, even more than his words, imparted his experience of the sacrificial love of Jesus on the cross. His glorious stammering about Love and the cross might only convey its fuller meaning to one who understands the nature of intellectual vision. In this direct encounter with God one is transformed. Yet, one is not complacent in this experience because there is also the knowledge that one must be transformed from glory to glory. For all eternity this transformation will never be complete, will never become boring and will never make us essentially equal to God. The mutuality and equality experienced are gifts given by God, but not deserved. Isn't every gift of love something that is not deserved, something not to be grasped at or clung to? Therefore, a profound detachment and humility necessarily accompanies an intellectual vision. Since God is *without form*, the face of Jesus may alert one to the importance of this *sovereign gift*.[48] The only way to experience the nature of God is to allow our faculties to become receptive to that which is 'formless' in the dark night of the spirit. Spiritual directors often experience *resistance* to or do not recognize the *night of sense* so that the process of *transformation* is halted early on.

In chapters five and seven of *Love Beacons: God's gift of Prayer* we have three examples of stories which include an intellectual vision of God's grandeur. In the seventh dwelling places Teresa, herself, tells how she *knew God* clearly as three Persons, yet one God. Clare experiences God as *an interpenetration of Persons in Love*. Father John knows God

---

48   Ibid., 197.

as *unconditional love,* poured out perfectly *in the Person of Jesus on the cross.* Were we able to study the intellectual visions of the saints, we would find many more aspects of God's awesome nature which directly touched them, enabling them to perform the unique ministry they were called to.

The problem with coming to understand this is the inability to explain in human terms a *formless* experience. When she first began speaking about union with God in the fifth dwelling places, Teresa said that God desires that union with Him not be given in vain, but that those who have it enable others to catch fire from their fire.[49] It is ultimately valuable to learn all we can about the unconditional love of Jesus on the cross. Experiencing this love, even through another person, makes us want to return that love.

Seeing the Face of God

One of our favorite prayers from *The Spiritual Canticle of St. John of the Cross,* which was emphasized in Angie's class was this:

> *When you looked at me Your eyes imprinted your grace in me; For this you loved me ardently; And thus my eyes deserved to adore what they beheld in you.*[50]

This prayer brings together the transformative experience of Angie, Father John and Clare. It describes just how it happens that *the one Jesus looks at with love is transformed.* The description goes on to say we behold this beauty together as Jesus and the person now do everything together. They are not one in essence, but they are one in will.

Fr. Waaijman, returning to St. John of the Cross and William of St. Thierry, goes on to explain how we can share in the desire to *see the face of God.* This longing goes back as far as Old Testament times. *The self-communication of God by himself and by nothing else, is the purest definition of face.* For this the soul longs, that God will press his face

---

49   Ibid., 97.
50   Kavanaugh, *Spiritual Canticle in Complete works of John of the Cross,* stanza 32, 599.

towards its own in an eternal kiss of love, that is to say that the soul may become *one* spirit with God *by the unity of its will...*

> *May I be so transformed in beauty that I in beauty resemble You and both behold ourselves in your beauty, because I possess your very own beauty, so that when one sees the other, each discovers his own beauty in the other...May my beauty be your beauty and your beauty be my beauty. Then I shall be You in your beauty and You will be me in my beauty. So we shall behold each other in your beauty.* [51]

In this transforming union one sees everything, including oneself in God. In the union of love in this dwelling place, one arrives at a *substantial knowledge* by means of *intellectual vision* that can only be given by God himself. It is an experiential knowledge of his essence, which is love. Teresa does her best to explain the permanent element of an *intellectual vision*. She says that when they first come, there may be some imaginative element to catch one's attention. However, what is learned goes beyond entry through the doors of our senses or faculties.

It happens as instantly as Our Lord once appeared to His apostles through closed doors when He said, *pax vobis. What God communicates to the soul here in an instant is a secret so great and a favor so sublime- and the delight the soul experiences so extreme- that I don't know what to compare it to...The Lord wished to reveal for that moment...the glory of heaven:*

> *The spirit is made one with God...For since His Majesty is also spirit, He has willed to show His love for us by giving some persons under-standing of the point to which this love reaches so that we might praise His grandeur. For He has so desired to be joined with the creature that, just as those who are married cannot be separated, He doesn't want to be separated from the soul.*[52]

---

51   Kees Waaijman, "Transformation: A Key Word in Spirituality," *Studies in Spirituality:* Peeters, Belgium #8; 998, 27-28;30.
52   Kavanaugh, *Castle*, 178.

John of the Cross speaks of this knowledge and this union with God as *substantial* in this way: *Being the shadow of God, through this substantial transformation, it (the soul) performs in this measure in God and through God what He through Himself does in it. For the will of the two is now one will, and thus God's operation and the soul's are one.*[53] It is no wonder that good works, which result from God's mercy, can be poured out marvelously through the love of a truly transformed person. And so we all should desire to be transformed in love. We do not desire anything spectacular, but to be united with God in love, in one will.

Teresa gives an analogy of this union, which is permanent and wholly indifferent as to any other gift God may give. She says God has control over the shutters in the innermost dwelling place and The Holy Spirit alone opens or closes them. But the person knows that God is there and that they are united in love no matter how much light or darkness is present. An example might be given of people in an exercise class. Should the lights go out, a person already *knows* who is there. One finds it easy to keep on dancing regardless of the amount of light in the room.

In fact, in the seventh dwelling places there is no longer any dryness. It would be impossible to remain forever in the intensity of one's initial experience of *intellectual vision*. Experiencing God so directly one could not continue to live in this world among people or be engaged in anything else.[54] Soon it does seem that light and darkness are the same, so indifferent is the person to God's secondary graces. The well-known prayer of St. Ignatius applies here, *Give me only your love and your grace. These are enough for me.*

Signposts - Seventh Dwelling Places

Knowledge of the attributes or essence of God is had in the intellectual vision of the seventh dwelling places. One grows in the love of the cross. There is no more fear of death than of a gentle rapture. There

---

53 Kavanaugh, *John of the Cross Collected Works,* 706.
54 Kavanaugh, *Castle,* 176.

is no dryness in prayer and one can normally enter contemplation at will. Impulses of love do not hinder whatever one is doing. When all things are taken care of in the routine of daily life, silence and solitude will be preferred. In the Christian life one is always aware of the need for formal times of prayer both on the individual and community levels.

Spiritual Practices - Seventh Dwelling Places

All things are seen *in God.* This is a significant shift from seeing God in *all things.* The only spiritual practice is love, which participates in and is an overflow of God's love directly experienced. One has entered the *mystery of God.* It is easy to return there consciously when unoccupied with important matters of ministry or of personal need, including the need for rest. Habitual presence of God is had in the affairs of daily life. Work and prayer are easily united in one continuous act of love. One can do vocal and discursive prayer as part of one's ministry although it is really not one's own personal prayer as such.

There are usually no times of dryness or interior trials in prayer. Nor are there usually the physical side effects as in the ecstasy of the sixth dwelling places. As one acts in union with the uncreated Spirit there is fortitude in the challenges of life. The water now is that of the heavy rain. All one must do is to allow it to penetrate every fiber of one's being and ministry.

Conclusion

Teresa tells in chapter one of how the person is brought into these dwelling places. It is an entry into the spiritual marriage, which is covered in chapter two. It is easy to think of this as Jesus bringing one home to his family, the Trinity, in chapter one. In chapter two Teresa describes the final proposal of marriage. It is important that this invitation to *spiritual marriage* is made through the *Humanity of Jesus.* When she told us in the previous dwelling places not to take our eyes off Jesus, Teresa was aware that our final and complete union with God would be in and through Jesus.

In chapter three Teresa gives the many benefits of the marriage of the soul with Jesus. These include significant benefits cited in chapter three of the seventh dwelling places. Among them are a deep joy and desire to serve the Crucified seen in the poor and suffering. There is no longer a fear of death. It is seen as an extension of the presence of God experienced as a *gentle rapture* in this life. In place of interior trials and dryness there remains a tender love of Our Lord with a desire to be alone or occupied in serving the spiritual needs of others. As contemplation becomes integrated in all of life, there are gentle impulses of God's love. These movements of love do not disturb one from the business at hand. Since the faculties and senses are enjoying God's gift of prayer in these dwelling places, there is no fear of counterfeit. The side effects of ecstasy almost never happen, but the Lord lets this person know quite simply what is pleasing to Him. Contemplation can be entered *at will* by the bride in the seventh dwelling places.

When Teresa began to distinguish *imaginative* vision from an *intellectual* experience, she began also to make other distinctions. She speaks of the union of created spirit with uncreated Spirit. She distinguishes the *soul* of a human being from the *spirit*, which is the fine point of the soul. In these distinctions Teresa is close to the writings of St. Paul, who because of his own profound experience of Christ knew that his encounter with Christ was a *spirit* to *Spirit* encounter and beyond the ability of his human faculties.

In chapter four of the seventh dwelling places Teresa tells why she thinks the Lord of glory brings us to these dwelling places. The integration here is so that the active and contemplative life can work smoothly together. She advises us to fix our eyes on the Crucified and everything will become easy. Compared to Teresa and John of the Cross our religious experience is attenuated. Yet, we can learn to appreciate God's great mercy in all whatever gifts we have been given. We can be thankful especially for the gift of God's Self in unconditional love. Always, Teresa encourages us to practice virtue. The amazement one feels at what God does in these dwelling places is a great sign of God's mercy. Teresa calls God "His Majesty" throughout the other dwelling places. Here she calls God "The Lord of Glory." One never seems to be done as one is led from glory to glory. We are told the marriage of created spirit with uncreated Spirit continues and progresses for all eternity.

In conclusion it is crucial to remind our readers that the spiritual journey is significantly different for each of us. The guidelines offered in this book reflect the way that the Holy Spirit operates in general. The application of them to individuals requires prayer and discernment. Persons picking up *The Interior Castle* for the first time do not often realize that spiritual reading is not to be done as other reading. Our personal experience allows us to understand some parts better than others. The advice the author gives in reading this book is to eventually read *The Interior Castle* side by side with it. It is vital that one *follow the attraction of grace* in regard to inspiration. *Rest in* what has most meaning for you. Let go of the rest for now. After a time when you come back to it, perhaps another part of the text will inspire you. In all things regarding prayer it is wise to remember the words of Teresa, who advises us, "Do what best stirs you to love." For *Love Beckons* to each of us personally and differently.

Glossary of Terms

First Dwelling Places - The mercy of God

Castle - The human soul filled with grace

Mote - Area of sin surrounding the castle

Door to the Castle - Prayer

Self-Knowledge - As compared to bread, self-knowledge is *the food* to be eaten throughout the spiritual journey with every kind of prayer, however dainty.

Second Dwelling Places - Friendship with God

Perseverance - The virtue required to remain out of the mote and recollected in the castle, which is he soul.

Conversation - Dialogue with self, others and God. Spiritual direction or *pastoral guidance* may be a special kind of conversation helpful in staying on the right path.

Third Dwelling Places - Dryness and Trials

Fear of the Lord - The fear of offending God. Scruples may be one of the trials at the end of this dwelling place to be distinguished from a healthy fear of the Lord.

Humility - Humility is truth. Teresa always places the indwelling presence of God in the human soul as the basis for humility. She sees as false - humility the position held by many that all are not called to union with God in this life.

Fourth Dwelling Places - Supernatural Prayer

Prayer of Recollection - Teresa distinguishes between the active prayer of recollection, which one does at will and the supernatural prayer of recollection known for the first time in the fourth dwelling places. Supernatural recollection draws one inward and is the entry to the prayer of quiet.

Prayer of Quiet - The prayer in which the Holy Spirit holds the will of the person in union. It has a dry or arid form and sweet form. In the dry form the faculties may be disruptive. Teresa referred to them as *wild horses.* In the sweet form one experiences brief times of spiritual delight.

Spiritual Delight –The result of the direct touch of God in contemplation. Spiritual Delight is different from the consolations in discursive prayer found in meditation through one's own effort. The person is more detached as one knows that one cannot arrive at contemplation through personal effort.

Contemplative Prayer - This term is correctly applied to any prayer which deliberately *disposes one for contemplation.* It is not synonymous with contemplation.

Contemplation - Prayer which according to Teresa of Avila and John of the Cross is the direct action of God and cannot normally be produced at will. Teresa makes an exception saying that *the bride* in the seventh dwelling places can enter into this prayer *at will.*

Contemplative Prayer Groups - Those groups which teach a method known as the prayer of simplicity. Anyone who knows the basics of the faith and stays close Christian Scripture may simplify their prayer. It is important that the groups are that foster it are not rigid and that they follow the sound teaching of Teresa of Avila and John of the Cross. Some Christian leaders who have been invested in contemplative prayer group movements today are:

The Benedictines, Thomas Keating,

John Main and Lawrence Freeman;

Mary Jo Meadows, SFCC, D. Min.

Fifth Dwelling Places - Prayer of Union

Incipient Union - Union of all the faculties for brief periods of time, no more than half an hour.

Death to Self - Using the image of the silkworm, building its cocoon, Teresa explains our death to self and rising in Christ.

Maintaining Quiet Within - Teresa uses the terms 'dove' and 'little white butterfly' to explain the excitement of the person having found God. One must be careful in these dwelling places not to lose this fire while trying to spread it to others. Later in the sixth dwelling places there will be no such danger.

Desire to remain in the Presence of God - Alternating states of prayer between the prayer of union and the prayer of quiet mark these dwelling places. Enlightened guidance is important so that one does not turn back thinking permanent union with God is impossible. Teresa values a director of considerable knowledge even more than a pious one.

Sixth Dwelling Places - Betrothal

Betrothal - Teresa describes these dwelling places in terms of a time of engagement where two persons contemplating marriage really get to know each other. Although marriage of a person with God is a thousand leagues superior, Teresa can think of no better analogy.

Trials - The gift of fortitude grows through interior and exterior trials which abound in these dwelling places.

Awakening - Spiritual awakening comes suddenly when least expected, fortifying and purifying a person for the remainder of the journey. An awakening can even be had by children. There is no age limit. The youngest known has been first grade. At times children can know in an instant what they will do for the rest of their lives. Or, for example, a parent prays for a teen and an awakening puts one of them on the right track with Jesus.

Locutions - Word or words which may be a valid inspiration of the Holy Spirit, but are subject to error. They may be heard as normal words are, from the outside hearing apparatus of the body or from deep within. They normally produce their effect immediately. Should they give a directive as to some external action, they should be taken to an experienced spiritual director for discernment.

Ecstasy - The effects of the divine operation extended even to the physical senses. As in death, it seems that the last sense to be held in suspension is hearing. Rapture is that form of ecstasy in which the mysteries of God are revealed. Ecstasy is a form of prayer which may last a long time. It seems like a very short time, due to the intense absorption of the faculties and senses in God. Teresa mentions three types of ecstasy: simple ecstasy, rapture and flight of the spirit.

Flight of the Spirit - In this divine operation a person will feel swiftly carried off, sometimes seeing their body as if suspended far above it. When these experiences are valid there is always a peaceful infusion of God's presence, wisdom and knowledge of the divine mysteries. The person will long for solitude and to be in God's presence. This, as opposed to a psychic experience, which causes unrest and gives no evidence of the wisdom of the divine mysteries. There will be a longing to share these divine mysteries as far as possible.

Authenticity - An authentic religious experience will be clothed in a profound experience of God's presence. In spite of the many misunderstandings Teresa says a person experiences in these dwelling places there will be joy to the point of spiritual inebriation. Teresa and John of the Cross both use the spiritual 'wine cellar' as an image for the *inebriation* experienced in the sixth dwelling places.

Humility - Looking to Jesus, Mary and the saints is a positive sign of humility. Teresa says one expresses humility by accepting the 'favors' God gives to others even though they may not be our own.

Imaginative Visions - May have some spiritual significance, but are also subject to error. These experiences should not be sought and should be reported to an experienced director, if one is available. Like locutions, their normal benefit when valid is produced on the spot. A desire to talk about such experiences, especially in public, shows a lack of humility and is a definite sign that the experience is not a valid religious experience.

Intellectual Visions - Formless experiences *of the mystery of God*, which are so much beyond the human senses and faculties that they are confirmed in certitude and are not subject to error. Teresa was asked how she *knew* it was Jesus though she saw none of his features. She said she *just knew.* There is no way to explain a formless experience. God is without form. It is the only way to experience God.

Encouragement through Religious Experiences - Particularly in time of trial, the Lord may visit a person through any number of religious experiences to strengthen them. Some of these may be *imaginative* visions, fragrances, tears, locutions and levitation.

Painful Desire for God - At times in these dwelling places a person will have no comfort in the things of God or from companionship with others. The most sociable person on the Myers/Briggs will find companionship once enjoyed as unbearable. One finds *wounds of love,* either as fiery experiences or delicious blows. These are more desirable than the spiritual delights which began in the fourth dwelling places.

Seventh Dwelling Places - Spiritual Marriage

Soul - The faculties: memory, intellect and will are distinctive of the human soul. Animals do not have these faculties.

Spirit - The fine point of the human soul is the spirit, which is capable of union with God, who is uncreated Spirit.

Union with the Most Holy Trinity - Teresa began to distinguish the difference between soul and spirit when she spoke of union with the Trinity. This *intellectual vi*sion is had beyond the faculties and senses in the fine point of the spirit, where one is united to the uncreated Spirit of God.

Spiritual Marriage - The mutuality of an eternal union between God and the human soul is possible even in this life through *The Humanity of Jesus*, who in the seventh dwelling places initiates the spiritual or mystical marriage of the person with God.

Habitual Presence - St. John of the Cross tells us that only Mary, the Mother of Jesus had constant awareness of the presence of God. Those who arrive at the spiritual marriage have an habitual awareness of God to which they easily return whenever they are not occupied with important matters.

Integration - The breath of the Holy Spirit, Love of Father and Son is breathed within both the inner life of God and within the inner life of a Christian. This divine life is simultaneously breathed out in ministry. It is the nature of love to be unable to contain itself. The person in union with God prays in the words of John of the Cross' *Spiritual Canticle*, "Come breathe *through* my garden and let your fragrance flow." The purpose of the spiritual marriage is good works performed through union with God and the action of the Holy Spirit.

Suggested Reading

Johnston, William, S.J., ed. *The Cloud of Unknowing,* (by an unknown English Mystic), Image Books, Doubleday, N.Y., 1973.

Kavanaugh K., O.C.D. and Rodriquez, O., O.C.D., trans., *Collected Works of John of the Cross,* Washington , D. C., ICS, 1991.

_____. Teresa of Avila, *The Interior Castle* in The Classics of Western Spirituality, New Jersey: Paulist Press, 1979.

Underhill, Evelyn, *Mysticism: A Study in the Nature and Development of Man's Spiritual Consciousness,* New York: Dover, 2002.

Lightning Source UK Ltd.
Milton Keynes UK
UKOW05f0124151016

285266UK00002B/171/P